REACHING HOME

To Lee –
A great attorney and
an even greater friend — thanks
for helping me "reach home".
Bob
1997

REACHING HOME

Pacific Salmon, Pacific People

PHOTOGRAPHS AND CAPTIONS BY NATALIE FOBES

Essays by Tom Jay and Brad Matsen

ALASKA NORTHWEST BOOKS™

ANCHORAGE ▪ SEATTLE ▪ PORTLAND

To the salmon and her people; may the saga continue.

And to my family, parents Virginia and Vernon, brothers Clark and Scott,

sisters Amy and Deb, and all my wonderful nieces and nephews.

—N. F.

Second printing 1995

Library of Congress Cataloging-in-Publication Data:
Fobes, Natalie. 1954—
       Reaching home : Pacific salmon, Pacific people / photographs and captions by Natalie Fobes : essays by Tom Jay and Brad Matsen.
           p.   cm.
       Includes bibliographical references (p.139) and index.
       ISBN 0-88240-449-0
       1. Pacific salmon. 2. Pacific salmon fisheries. 3. Salmon fishing. 4. Fishery conservation. 5. Endangered species.
       I. Jay, T. E., 1943— . II. Matsen, Bradford. III. Title.
       QL638.S2F63 1994
       333.95 '6—dc20   94-25182
                                                                                                              CIP

Editor: Ellen Harkins Wheat
Designer: Elizabeth Watson
Map: Vikki Leib
Salmon illustration: Marvin Oliver

Photos:
       Front cover and title page: Sockeye salmon swim in a lake near Bristol Bay, Alaska.
       Back cover: A salmon returns to its home stream in British Columbia, Canada.
       Frontispiece (facing page): Male spawning sockeye salmon develop hooked jaws and humped backs.
       Pages 6-7: A chinook salmon struggles against the current in a Washington stream.
       Page 10: Spawning salmon are highlighted by the sun.
       Page 11: An endangered Snake River sockeye alevin.

Alaska Northwest Books ™
An imprint of Graphic Arts Center Publishing Company
Editorial office: 2208 NW Market Street, Suite 300, Seattle, WA 98107
Catalog and order dept.: P.O. Box 10306, Portland, OR 97210
       800-452-3032

Printed on acid-free paper in the United States of America

CONTENTS

PHOTOGRAPHER'S PREFACE

MY OBSESSION WITH PACIFIC SALMON began in 1983 before I had turned thirty. Now I am closer to forty, and the salmon haunt me still. Many times I thought I was done with the story, but a phone call or

a letter or a dream would pull me back in. Sometimes I think that I didn't choose to do the story of salmon but rather the salmon chose me. And I remember the day that happened.

It was a blue-sky October day, and birch leaves were splattered on the gravel. I was recovering from ankle surgery and Dad had taken time off from his engineering job to take care of me. After two days of soap operas and game shows, he insisted that we go for a ride. We headed south from Seattle toward a river where I had heard there were salmon spawning. It seemed like a good Northwestern thing to do.

When we reached the stream, Dad protectively held my arm as I hobbled along the shaded path. We joined the people crowding at the fence that separated them from the river. They pointed and clapped, laughed, then whispered with tones normally used in church.

A streak of crimson split the seams of the waterfall; I leaned forward to clear the fence from my sight. Two more streaks; another. And then—a sockeye salmon floated in the air.

Even today it is hard to describe the jumble of emotions I experienced during those moments. My entire being was drawn up short. I was excited, filled with exuberance yet strangely calmed and comforted. It was like running with my horse before a storm when the electricity of unspent energy tickles the follicles of your hair. I stopped thinking; I started being.

I remember slowly turning to my father. His face had a look I had never seen, and before he turned away I saw his eyes were full of tears.

What is it about the salmon that touches a person's soul? Dad was not a scientist, and he didn't know the incredible life story of the salmon. He wasn't a fisherman, and he had never seen a salmon before that afternoon. This Minnesota farmer's son was not really a sportsman, although he had hunted with my brothers when they were younger. My father did not—maybe could not—share his thoughts and feelings with me. And as my mind returned to the image of the leaping salmon, I was surprised at the intensity of my own feelings. After all, it was just a fish.

For more than a decade, I have lived with the people of the salmon off and on—Northwest Indians, commercial and sport fishermen, biologists, salmon ranchers and farmers, Russians, Ainu, and Japanese. They all use the fish for different reasons, but the salmon is more than a commodity. It is a theme that cascades relentlessly through their spirits. When asked to explain it, they often fall quiet, shrug their shoulders, embarrassed, and say "Well, you know," before changing the subject.

I do know what they are trying to reach. When I am asked why I have spent the past eleven years of my life photographing and writing about the world of salmon, I struggle to find the words that describe this natural symbiosis. This relationship is as inherent to me as breathing and just as hard to describe.

And so I respond with slices of truth, examining each one as I lay it on the table. Maybe it's because of all nature's stories, the salmon's sacrifice is one of the most compelling, I say. Or, since ancient times the salmon has shaped the cultures of the Pacific Rim. Maybe it's just that I like the people of the salmon. Or, maybe, I say as I shrug my shoulders, it's the mystery. I love the fact that salmon have successfully kept their biggest secret. We still don't know how Pacific salmon, swimming thousands of miles out in the ocean, find their way back to their home streams. I wonder if we ever will.

The enigma of the salmon has remained a constant in my ever-changing life. My father died a couple of years after we stood together at the waterfall on that beautiful October day. And my work has led me far from the streams of the salmon. But I always return.

Maybe I am a pessimist. Or maybe I know too much about the animals we call human. But I fear for the future of the wild salmon, especially in the Northwest and British Columbia. Run after run in stream after stream is disappearing, not from any official plan to exterminate them but rather from the outdated and erroneous idea that we as individuals cannot harm a species as great as the Pacific salmon. We can. And we have.

I hope I never live in a time when my home streams lie silent and barren, when I must travel to remote reaches of Alaska and Canada and Russia to see them spawn. The ache of their absence would remain with me forever.

—N. F.

"An Indian gave me a piece of fresh salmon, roasted, which I ate with relish. This was the first salmon I had seen and convinced me we were in the waters of the Pacific."

Journals of
Meriwether Lewis,
August 1805

INITIATION

The Storied Waters of the North Pacific

TOM JAY

YEARS AGO I WORKED AS A BOAT PULLER on a troller fishing the Fairweather grounds, west of Glacier Bay, Alaska. We were newcomers to Alaska. The skipper, Larry Scoville, was an old friend and seasoned Northern California troller. We were fishing a new boat with a new diesel, so Larry and I spent a few days in the fjords and passes around Elfin Cove rehearsing the gear, the boat, and crew. We were testing FV *Sinara* for any quirky motions, vibrations, or noises that might spook the wily salmon. Larry watched my side of the boat, counting the fish caught, and warned me if the salmon didn't like my smell I'd have to wear gloves when I baited leaders or changed "hoochy" lures. The *Sinara* worked, and I was confirmed a bare-handed boat puller. We caught a scatter of silvers and kings, and headed for the Fairweather grounds and the chance to catch some big king salmon.

The second day on the grounds, Larry had us fishing frenetically on a school of stout king salmon. In the midst of the blood-slippery melee, Larry called me to bring the landing net to his side of the boat. He was working a tremendous king salmon on a rubber snubber we called the kill line, and gave me instructions on how to approach the salmon with the net.

It was the biggest king I had seen that summer—slab-sided, thick-bodied, and five feet long, perhaps a 100-pounder. As I brought the net behind and under it, it began to swim away—not fast, but steadily, like a draft animal pulling a heavy load. The kill line went taut and the 100-pound test leader snapped as the great fish flashed out of sight. This story is a reminder that salmon is free and that the musings that follow are only lines and hooks that hold it momentarily.

THE SEASON WAS A BUST. The silvers were late and the kings hit and miss, so I quit before the season ended and went south to Seattle to study and work. It was seven years before I saw another free salmon. Settled with my family in the Olympic Peninsula community of Chimacum, Washington, one frosty winter evening I walked to the modest alder-lined creek that winds through the pasture south of our place. Lost in the icy stillness, I was startled by a sudden, staccato splashing. Whatever it was gathered its energy in quiet, then burst forward again, closer, moving up the creek. I crept to the cattle bridge to glimpse this night visitor.

PREVIOUS PAGES:

◄ ◄ *With the Columbia River as a backdrop, Darrell Jack swings a chinook salmon from his boat to his truck. For generations the Yakima Indians have fished the Columbia River and its tributaries. Explorer William Clark wrote about a village near this point in his journal in 1805: "I saw several large scaffolds on which the Indians dry fish. I counted 107 stacks of dried pounded fish . . . which must have contained 10,000 pounds of neat fish." The 1974 Boldt decision guaranteed treaty tribes in Washington state half the harvestable fish. As the runs become smaller, the number of salmon Native Americans can catch is declining as well.*
◄ *Salmon fillets dry in a smokehouse on the banks of the Columbia River. In this day of supermarkets and fast food, Indians of the Northwest, Canada, and Alaska still depend on the salmon for a large part of their diet.*

◄ A fin is all that is visible from the carcass of a chinook salmon on Canada's Adams River.

In the ice-blue light of winter, a salmon flourished, dorsal fin and back just breaking the easy iridescent ripples of the stream. Another dark, sparkling dash and it was below me in a log-dammed pool. It was a large wild male coho, smoky red and silver in his spawning regalia. Migrating at night while hunters dream, the salmon had followed the scent of this creek home, a pilgrimage repeated faithfully by his ancestors since the last ice age.

Witnessing the homecoming of this ancient being, the salmon, so precise, practiced, and generous in his longing, quickened my own sense of homecoming. I felt lost and found at the same time—squinting into the polished darkness of the water, afraid to lose that timely guide. In that numinous moment on the bridge, salmon became my teacher. He has kindled and animated my curiosity and I have followed salmon into the haunted waters of watersheds and folklore. Since that night on the bridge, the salmon have been swimming in my dreams.

INITIATION

SALMON ARE BORN IN BROOKS, creeks, rills—the headwaters of greater streams. They run to the sea for a miraculous sojourn. Feasting, their flesh reddens in the richness of the sea. Mature, they awaken to the call of their natal waters, and follow clues subtle and disparate as magnetic fields and the bouquet of stones to the streams of their birth to spawn and die. Loving and dying in home ground is a primordial urge. Salmon embody this for us, our own loving deaths at home in the world. Salmon dwell in two places at once, in our hearts and in the waters, and they know the way home.

ONCE NEARLY EVERY WATERSHED around the North Pacific Rim, from San Diego, California, to Kyushu Island in southern Japan, supported one or more runs of Pacific salmon (king, sockeye, pink, chum, coho, steelhead, masu, and amago). Each run or stock of salmon fits itself over eons to local conditions, its adaptability tempered by ice ages, floods, and droughts. The vital beauty of salmon has been shaped by the infinite refinements of necessity. The salmon's genius is in making friends with fate. The king salmon of the Elwha River in Washington, for example, have evolved to enormous size, up to six feet and 100 pounds, because females must be powerful enough to excavate spawning beds (redds) below the scour depth of this steep and highly energized river.

The myriad life histories and the fine and grand morphological differences the salmon have evolved over thousands of years might be imagined as embodiments of watershed character—the salmon an expression, a vernacular of the watershed. Logically and poetically, the salmon are the soul of the watershed, its glory. Salmon are, as salmon restoration herald Freeman House announced thirty years ago, the totem of the North Pacific Rim. Freeman

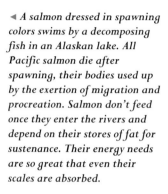

◄ A salmon dressed in spawning colors swims by a decomposing fish in an Alaskan lake. All Pacific salmon die after spawning, their bodies used up by the exertion of migration and procreation. Salmon don't feed once they enter the rivers and depend on their stores of fat for sustenance. Their energy needs are so great that even their scales are absorbed.

was restating a wisdom familiar to the indigenous peoples of the North Pacific Rim. The Yurok of California and the Ainu of Japan, while separated by thousands of miles of ocean, celebrated the salmon as a vital element of their cosmos. In many regions the human culture coevolved with the salmon, because both species—*Homo sapiens* and *Oncorhynchus*—were recolonizing the post-glacial barrens at the same time.

In the rub of weather and landscape, Native peoples and salmon adapted behaviors to fit local conditions. As the glaciers retreated, strays from refuge salmon populations began to probe the meltwater rivers and streams that drained the tundra landscapes of the glacial wake. Periodic heavy glacial outwash could wipe out generations of salmon and limit the success of salmon forays into new watersheds. While the persistent salmon fertilized the raw waters of glacial watersheds, plant communities migrating north and south from unglaciated botanical preserves were gradually reestablishing conifers in the post-glacial landscape. It was this "conspiracy" of salmon and trees that transformed and stabilized the watersheds of the North Pacific.

Large conifers provided shade, stream structure, and a detritus-based aquatic food chain that nurtured the various species of Pacific salmon. Salmon runs moved tons of sediment downstream and helped stabilize river channels. Salmon also returned ocean-gathered nutrients to the rain-leached and glacially plowed soils of much of the North Pacific. As spawning and spawned-out salmon were retrieved from streams by bear, otter, eagle, raven, and others, their nutrients were distributed throughout the forest.

A local forester once took me to a gargantuan grandmother fir, regal still in a mature second-growth forest. Four large people holding hands could barely encircle its girth. Its wind-blasted top was crowned with an active osprey nest. While we all craned our necks to view the nest, the forester pointed to the foot of the tree and asked what we saw. Around the base of the tree were tracks and scat of all kinds—coyote, raccoon, bear, deer, squirrel. "You

IT WAS THIS "CONSPIRACY" OF SALMON AND TREES THAT TRANSFORMED AND STABILIZED THE WATERSHEDS OF THE NORTH PACIFIC.

▶ *High over the Chilkat River near Haines, Alaska, a bald eagle feasts on a salmon head.*

see," he said, "the young osprey are much like our children when they dump their oatmeal off the high chair, except here the dropped food (salmon) is mopped up by a host of creatures, even deer and squirrel, who nibble the bones for calcium." This great fir, miles from any salmon creek, was a distribution point for forest nutrients. By dropping salmon from the treetops, the osprey were providing a welcome feast for the savvy creatures below. Seen in this light, salmon is a current between the forest and the sea. Salmon is a sea-bright silver shuttle weaving the rain-green world of the temperate Pacific watersheds.

ABOUT 5,000 YEARS AGO, when salmon were established and abundant, Native peoples would move seasonally to fishing camps along streams and feast. But when the runs were over, the people had to move on after other food, for they had yet to develop food preservation techniques to take full advantage of the salmon bounty.

Once Native peoples mastered salmon food preservation, they settled in permanent villages near preferred fishing sites. They learned through overharvest and calamity-induced famine to manage the salmon resource at maximum sustainable yield. Pre-contact native cultures were probably harvesting more salmon than nineteenth- and twentieth-century industrial fisheries. Some researchers estimate that Native harvest of salmon in the Pacific Northwest had been reduced ninefold before the large influx of European pioneers. The thundering "walk-across" runs reported by early European settlers were likely the result of tribal populations being decimated by the epidemics and whiskey that announced European eminence.

In pre-contact times, by working diligently during the salmon season a family could store in a few months enough fish to meet its basic food requirements for a year. Of course there were supplemental foods—whale, fowl, shellfish, and plants, berries, and seaweed—but the fundamental food resource was salmon. It was the axis of their economy and for many the

Robes and boots made of salmon skin, hooks and points made of bone, and salmon vertebrae were unearthed at village sites in the Russian Far East and prove the importance of salmon not only to the early indigenous peoples of North America but also to those of Asia. At the Kamchatka Peninsula village of Ushki, Russian archaeologist Nikolai N. Dikov has unearthed salmon bones and ceremonial artifacts that are more than 11,000 years old.

► *A salmon makes her way up a Canadian stream more than 100 miles from the ocean. In Canada and throughout the Northwestern states, the pristine stream ecosystem is being devastated by logging, farming, and development. Without cool, clean, fresh-flowing water, the salmon cannot survive.*

22

SALMON IS A SEA-BRIGHT

SILVER SHUTTLE WEAVING

THE RAIN-GREEN WORLD

OF THE TEMPERATE

PACIFIC WATERSHEDS.

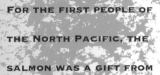

FOR THE FIRST PEOPLE OF
THE NORTH PACIFIC, THE
SALMON WAS A GIFT FROM
HIDDEN BUT
PRESCIENT POWERS.

hub of their culture. The salmon's abundance gave early peoples leisure, the time to develop the refined and distinct cultures of the North Pacific Coast.

GIVEN THEIR LONG ASSOCIATION with salmon and its importance to them, it is no wonder that original peoples developed a deep and coherent connection to salmon. We moderns love salmon; it is the choice food of our region. But to the first peoples of the North Pacific, salmon was not merely food, it was energy. It was not energy in our sense of Btu's or calories, but was what William Blake meant when he said energy is eternal delight. Native peoples' close relations with salmon had worn through to a kind of intuitive essence: the salmon was the animate representative of greater powers, a fellow being in this fateful universe.

Many peoples of the North Pacific honored salmon on its yearly return home. They imagined salmon as a representative of the other side, the world where the powers of creation reside. To the Ainu, Gilyak, and Chukchi of Northeast Asia, the salmon was representative of the sea spirit. To the tribes of the Northwest Coast, it was a supernatural human being whose village was in the sea and who put on the salmon disguise as a gift to honor the respect the local people showed his salmon people.

In the Native cosmos, salmon can choose to present itself in abundance or not at all. This vision required special treatment for the salmon. When the S'Klallam of Beecher Bay, British Columbia, caught the first sockeye salmon, little children sprinkled their hair with sacred white eagle down, painted their faces, and put on white blankets. They met the canoe and carried the first salmon in their arms as if it were an infant. An older woman cleaned the fish with a mussel-shell knife, after which the flesh was boiled and given to the children to eat. To the S'Klallam, the sockeye is a person and deserves careful treatment. Versions of the first salmon ceremony were practiced by Native peoples from California to Japan. The salmon

◄ For centuries in ceremonies around the Pacific Rim, indigenous peoples have celebrated the return of the salmon. Tulalip Indian Raymond Moses tunes his drum before joining in the first fish ceremony held at the reservation near Marysville, Washington. This traditional feast was revived in the 1970s and is now an annual event.

was treated as a respected guest before it was eaten, so that when the salmon spirits returned to their watery villages they would report that their gifts had been honorably received.

For the first people of the North Pacific, the salmon was a gift from hidden but prescient powers. The salmon was sacramental food, and the proper attitude was to feast on its energy in gratitude and repay its generosity by respectful treatment. You couldn't have your cake unless you ate it in gratitude. The Chukchi of Kamchatka ate the first salmon caught themselves; they wouldn't sell it to their Russian masters. You can't have your cake and sell it too. The Gilyak of Sakhalin Island, north of Hokkaido, Japan, had a special language for speaking to salmon and other game. The Koryak of Siberia had a story called "Fish Woman" in which a man marries a fish woman, and though she is loving and patient, the mistreatment she receives in his house causes her to leave and take her relatives with her. This story echoes a Northwest Coast Tsimshian tale wherein a man mistreats his wife, "Salmon Woman," who returns to the sea with her silvery familiars. Native relations with the salmon resource required the same care and attention as marriage. Both were crucial to survival.

◄ Dressed in traditional clothing and marked with an Ainu mouth tattoo, Sute Orita carries the symbolic first fish to begin the salmon ceremony in Sapporo, Japan. Banned from fishing almost a century ago by the Japanese, the Ainu are working to regain rights to the salmon.

In the autumn, the Ainu of Japan watched for the magnolia leaves to fall because it presaged the arrival of the chum salmon. When they took the first salmon from the river, they passed it through a special game window in their house and honored the salmon ritually in front of the hearth fire. In their world, fire could see and report back to the supernatural world the hospitable treatment of the salmon. The Ainu also had a ceremony to bid the salmon spirits farewell when, in their human form, they paddled their canoes back to their homes in the supernatural world.

These beliefs are a deep recognition and affirmation of the place of the human imagination in nature. Native legend is a well-spoken alchemy of soul and landscape, each story informed by a thousand tellings. The wisdom of Native peoples is to live in and husband a world wherein nature and its beings hold humans responsible for their actions.

INITIATION

I ONCE SWAM DOWN WASHINGTON'S DUCKABUSH RIVER in wet suit and mask. It was during the dog salmon run and there was a flood of fish in the river. The current ran both ways that day. Halfway down the river I floated over a deep pool where an eddy had piled a pyramid of golden alder leaves. Further on, resting in the shallows and musing on what I'd seen, I noticed a shape move behind a submerged snag. It was a large male dog salmon, splotchy gray and yellow with faint copper tiger stripes; spawned out but alive in his eyes. I dove and glided toward him until we were a foot apart. I looked into his eye. He saw me but did not move. I was just another river shadow, an aspect of his dying. He was crossing over to the other side, watershed specter feeding the firs, subterranean sometime king, tree-born elder, tutor.

◄ *A female salmon swims beneath the surface of a Canadian stream. As the trees lose their leaves, these salmon finish their lives.*

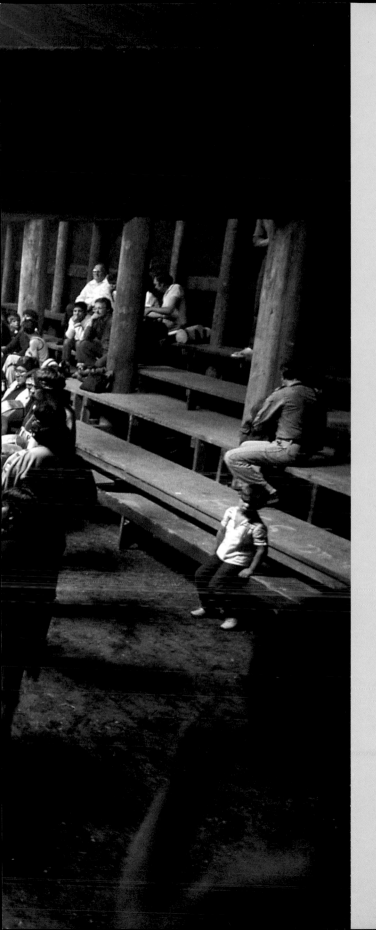

TRADITIONS

Natalie Fobes

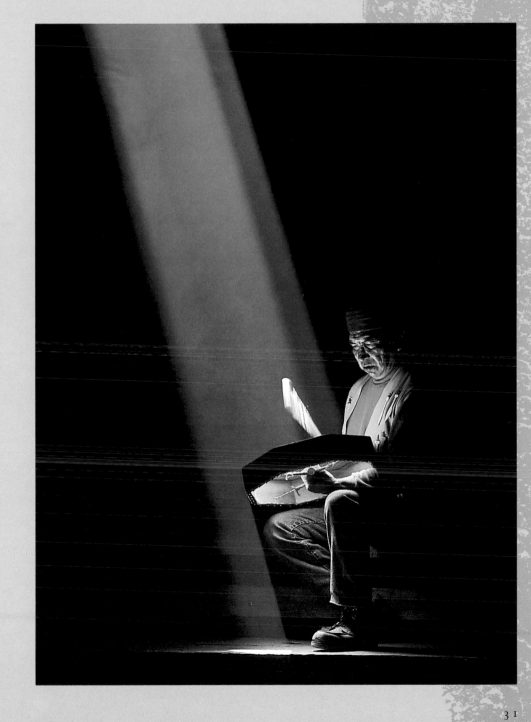

THE SALMON ARE A GIFT from the Creator, the tribal elders told me, a

gift from the Spirit who made the water and all creatures of the water,

the banks of the river, the berries and roots, the mammals and birds. If

people treat the salmon with respect and honor, the fish will return

from their mansion beneath the horizon at the bottom of the ocean to

sacrifice themselves so mankind can survive.

PREVIOUS PAGES:

◄◄◄ *In a tradition that dates back to ancient times, the Tulalip Indians celebrate the first fish ceremony on their reservation near Marysville, Washington, each June.*
◄◄ *Captured by a beam of smoky sunlight, Raymond Moses tunes his drum in the longhouse before the first fish ceremony.*

FACING PAGE:

◄ *Singing a song of welcome, Tulalip tribal members gently*

carry a salmon from the water to the longhouse. While tradition holds that the first fish caught by the tribe is honored, the modern-day reality of smaller runs and shortened fishing seasons dictates that the "first" salmon is often bought from a coastal tribe.

▲ *A well-worn drum used for tribal celebrations is painted with the symbols of the legendary salmon, bear, and orca whale.*
► *Knowledge and tradition are passed from generation to generation during the first fish ceremony.*

THOUSANDS OF MILES ACROSS the Pacific Ocean from the Northwest's Tulalip Indians, Japan's indigenous people, the Ainu, also believed the salmon were people who sacrificed themselves for mankind. Dependent on the return of salmon for food, the Ainu were almost wiped out at the beginning of the century when the Japanese stopped their fishing and blocked Hokkaido and Honshu rivers to trap the returning salmon. To this day, the Japanese government has refused to lift this ban, and only in the past few years have the Ainu been allowed to catch salmon for ceremonial purposes. Recently the Ainu have begun to reclaim their traditions and have revived the first fish ceremony.

▲ During the first fish ceremony in Sapporo, Japan, Ainu present food and drink to the gods who they believe reside in the ornately carved sticks.
▶ Fermented rice wine is shared by the celebrants during the first fish ceremony.

▶ ▶ Ainu come to Sapporo from all over the island of Hokkaido to take part in the two-day celebration of their culture. The Ainu continue to petition the Japanese government for restoration of fishing rights.

YAKIMA INDIAN MIKE GEORGE was tired as he trudged up the bank after fishing all night in the shadow of The Dalles Dam on the Columbia River in Washington state. He didn't have much to show for his effort— only two fish. In the old days it used to be a pretty good fishing spot, but the dam's currents have destroyed the pools where salmon rested before ascending the river.

This morning he is angry. "People accuse the Indians of not looking toward the future," he told me, "of not saving money in the bank or taking out insurance or making retirement plans. But we did plan ahead. The Indian people preserved the earth and her creatures for future generations. Hundreds of years ago our ancestors were planning ahead for you and for me so there would be a world for all of us."

▶ *Dwarfed by The Dalles Dam, a Yakima fisherman dipnets from his platform on the Columbia River. Beneath the dam's reservoir lies Celilo Falls, which was once a traditional salmon fishing camp and a center of commerce for Northwest Indians. Each spring tribes traveled here from the shores of the Pacific Ocean, over the Olympic and Cascade mountains, and from the plains of what are now Washington, Oregon, Montana, and Idaho to trade shells, quills, berries, skins, meat, and salmon. In 1953, this rich fishing site was covered by the dammed river.*

WHEN THE FIRST SWALLOWS WING *their way through the Columbia River*

Gorge, the spring chinook make their way up the rivers and Yakima

fishermen return to the Klickitat River near Lyle, Washington, to fish the

old way—from platforms hung precariously over rapids with dip nets

attached to poles.

◄ *With declining runs, fishing gets pretty slow. To make the hours go faster, Wade Porter (left) and Durwin Lumley play backgammon.*
▲ *The locations of Native fishing platforms are handed down from father to son, and with the location comes the knowledge of the river's bottom and the hidey-holes where salmon lie. Dusk and night are the best times to fish, Dave Leonard, Sr., told me as his son fished below. The salmon*

can't see your shadow and they can't see your net. But it is a dangerous time to fish. On moonless nights fishermen sometimes step off the platform's edge. Each season two or three fishermen are lost to the river.
► *Glen George rests while keeping watch over his net. Dip net fishing is hard work. Holding the heavy thirty-four-foot-long net and leaning over the river makes your back muscles spasm and your arms shake.*

◄◄ *In the glow of twilight, a Quinault Indian tends his gill net stretched partway across the Quinault River on Washington's coast near Cape Elizabeth.*
◄ *Young Melissa Cheney helps her father, Benjamin, fish on the Quinault reservation near Taholah, Washington. Quinault sockeye salmon, nicknamed "bluebacks," are renowned for their delicious flavor, which many say comes from the high oil content of the flesh.*
▼ *Darrell Jack rests after clearing his net of salmon on the Columbia River.*

FROM THE TOWER

The Evolution and Biology of Pacific Salmon

BRAD MATSEN

MOST YOUNG SALMON BIOLOGISTS put in a few seasons
aloft, like clipper-ship lookouts, staring down through the
rain and mosquitoes to count spawners in wilderness rivers.
Typically, a counting tower looks like an aluminum and ply-
wood parody of a lunar lander, and the work is primitive,
tedious, and usually left to graduate students. On Alaska's

Naknek River, for instance, a rickety scaffold as tall as a city phone pole rises each spring on the up-sun bank of a muddy tundra oxbow about half a mile down from the mother lake. Every half hour, during the long days and white nights of the arctic summer, some tired rookie biologist poles a skiff across the river from camp, climbs the tower, and counts with a chrome doorkeeper's tallywhacker for precisely five minutes. Because the sockeye invoke camouflage against bears and other predators during this last, urgent stretch of their saga of thousands of miles from the river, into the Pacific Ocean, and back, the counting teams stake white panels to the streambed for better visibility. Against that unlikely brightness, the salmon appear and vanish, shadow fish in a rush for home, creation, and a death as poignant and graceful as any on earth. Spent, they rot quickly in pathetic tatters, their bodies surrendering the nourishment they have carried from the sea to the watershed.

Later, at a desk somewhere, another biologist uses the half-hourly samples to estimate the number of sockeye that reached the lake and delivered their genetic messages. We count salmon with sonar, too, inbound and outbound from their streams and rivers, and we dissect them, observe them, analyze their scales, breed them, tag them, and electrically isolate their cells to classify them. We study their relationships with the water, land, and the critters they feed or eat. We decide how we will "manage the resource," how many salmon we will "harvest" for food or otherwise kill with the aim of leaving enough for succeeding generations. We presume to know enough about them to make such monumental decisions, but we haven't done well. Salmon, quite simply, seem to be allergic to people.

BY THE TIME OUR MOST ANCIENT PRIMATE ANCESTORS showed up 4 million years ago, members of the family *Salmonidae* had already been around for eons. The oldest undoubted fossil salmon is *Eosalmo driftwoodensis* (literally "dawn salmon"), a freshwater fish that lived during

PREVIOUS PAGES:

◄ ◄ *With heads pointed upstream, sockeye smolts in Alaska's Naknek River migrate downstream and are guided to the ocean by river currents. In two, three, or four years, these salmon will return as part of the world's greatest salmon run. Between 44 and 66 million fish return annually to the rivers that flow into Western Alaska's Bristol Bay.*

◄ *Suspended in a stream of light, sockeye salmon swim to their spawning grounds in a Canadian stream.*

► *Trapped in the roots of a streamside tree, a spawned-out salmon carcass will release nutrients back into the water, which will help nourish its progeny.*

PACIFIC SALMON
ARE ANADRAMOUS
—THE WORD MEANS
"UP-RUNNING"—
AND ALL BUT THE
STEELHEAD ARE
SEMELPAROUS.

the Eocene, 50 million years ago. During the late Miocene epoch, 5 to 6 million years ago, salmon were giants with fangs, great beasts ten feet long weighing 500 pounds we now call *Smilodonichthys rastrosus,* the sabertooth salmon. Sometimes you eat the fish, sometimes the fish eats you. Modern humans who look like us date back just 35,000 years or so; modern Pacific salmon, *Oncorhynchus,* emerged during the Pleistocene 2 million years ago, then as now creatures of the ice, rivers, and oceans.

◄ *The chinook's instinct to swim against the flow shows itself early in life.*

Georg Wilhelm Steller, the legendary German naturalist who sailed with Vitus Bering on his second voyage to North America in 1741–1742, was the first to list the species of Pacific salmon. The names he gave them are Russian in origin because Steller and Bering explored for the Tsar. In 1792, Johann Julius Wilbaum, a German ichthyologist, used Steller's notes to formally describe the members of the genus *Oncorhynchus: O. tshawytscha* (chinook); *O. kisutch* (coho); *O. nerka* (sockeye); *O. keta* (chum); *O. gorbuscha* (pink); and *O. masou* (cherry). Later, we described *O. amago* and *O. mykiss* (steelhead). Without human beings, salmon have no names, but because we are around to distinguish one from the other, their differences have become words and, to some of us, a litany: blackmouth-king-chinook and spring-tyee-hog and jack, coho-northern and silver, sockeye-blueback and red, chum and dog-calico-gila, pink and humpie, steelie and metalhead, masu-cherry-amago. We know them, too, by the seasons of their return, and the names of the rivers and tributaries to which they are bound as surely as red blood cells in arteries, veins, and capillaries. A sockeye is a sockeye, but, like dialects of the same language, a spring Copper River sockeye from Prince William Sound and a midsummer Naknek River red are subtly, but clearly, salmon with different accents.

Pacific salmon are anadromous—the word means "up running"—and all but the steelhead are semelparous. They are born in freshwater, migrate to the sea to mature, return to freshwater, and spawn. A fish that dies after spawning once is semelparous. Atlantic salmon, of the genus *Salmo,* are anadromous but not semelparous, and steelhead, too, spawn more than once. Catadromous fish—most notably freshwater eels—are "down-running" because they are born and reproduce in the ocean and mature in rivers and lakes. Salmon probably became anadromous to adapt to the cycles of ice and water that have dominated their range since the Pleistocene when they evolved to their present form in the cold, nutrient-poor freshwater of northern latitudes. From time to time, great glaciers completely hushed the continental rivers and lakes beneath crackling blankets of ice, and drove the fish to sea.

Salmon are among the quickest studies in the evolutionary drama, able to change so rapidly in just a few generations that geneticists favor them for experiments in mutation and adaptation. They evolved the physiological and biochemical traits necessary to migration, homing, and survival in both fresh- and saltwater, and further refined themselves into hundreds of races distinctly bound to specific watersheds. Every salmon is a member of not only its broad taxonomic species like king or coho, but of a natal subgroup from its particular stream or river, marked by distinct traits such as scale color, size, flesh color, and even taste to a predator.

Each species, and in some cases each race or run within a species, carries a schedule for fresh- and saltwater migration in its genetic code. Chinook salmon, adapted to long or steep rivers, build strength and size during as many as five years at sea after a year in freshwater. A seiner off Alaska caught a 145-pounder, though surely bigger chinooks have lived and live now.

The coho's anadromous rhythm is similar to the chinook's, its closest relative, though its sea time is shorter, usually only eighteen months or two years. If salmon were automobiles, cohos would be the sports cars, fast, agile, and compact. The biggest ones, late in the season when all the fattening is done, can weigh fifteen pounds, and anglers say catching a coho on a fly rod is sublime.

MODERN PACIFIC SALMON, *Oncorhynchus,* EMERGED DURING THE PLEISTOCENE 2 MILLION YEARS AGO, THEN AS NOW CREATURES OF THE ICE, RIVERS, AND OCEANS.

▶ *Their jaws hooked and bodies humped, hundreds of spawning pink salmon swim in a Russian trap. These salmon will be used as brood stock for a nearby hatchery.*

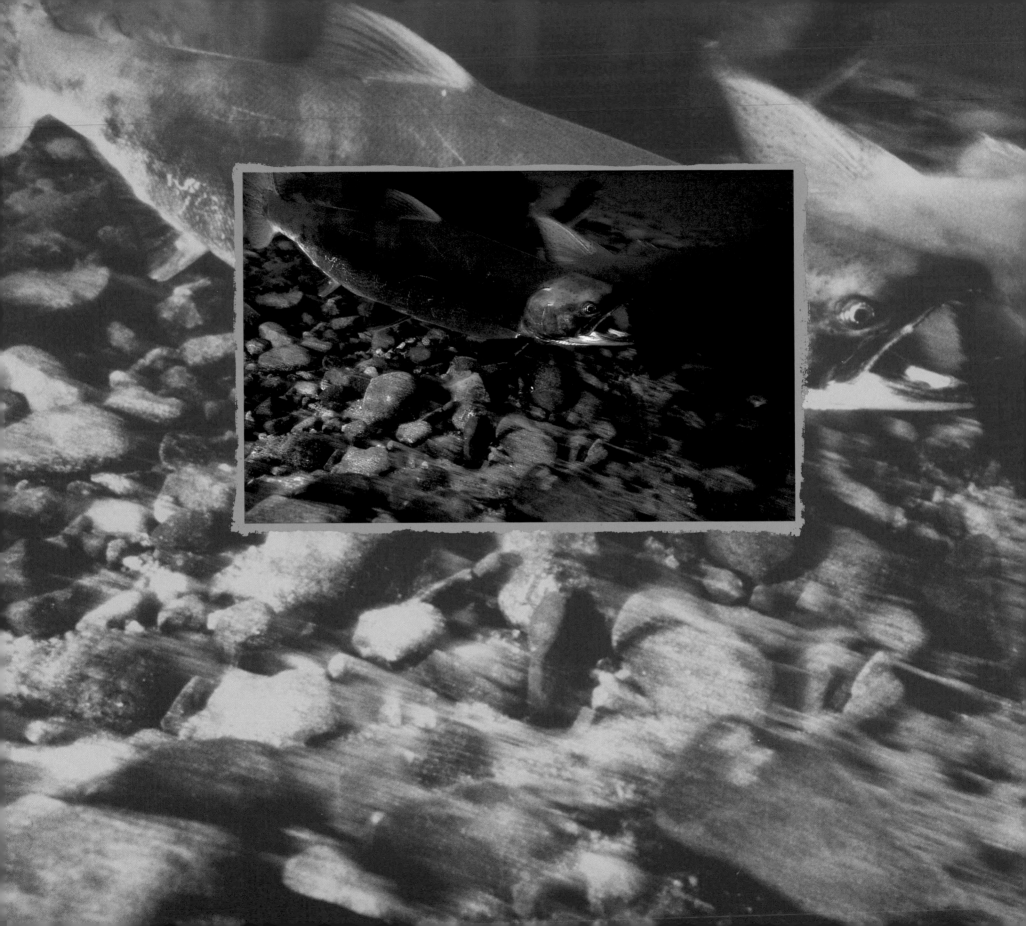

The annual cycles of the sockeye are the most varied of the tribe, from a few months to three years in freshwater, and from one to four years in the sea. Their life spans are so varied because they depend on more ecological combinations, patterns, and sizes of lakes, streams, and rivers than any other salmon. Some biologists spend their entire careers on the complicated sockeye, trying to predict the timing and size of the runs for commercial packers who want to know how much money to borrow to finance their seasons, and how much to pay the fishermen who always think it's not enough. (The kokanee, a close cousin of the sockeye, has even abandoned its anadromous instincts in favor of life as a smaller fish in landlocked lakes.)

◄ From the time her eggs are laid and fertilized until she dies, a female sockeye salmon will protect her nest from other fish and animals.

Chums are the blue-collar salmon, dependable, nothing fancy, the most widely distributed of all species, ranging from Korea around the Pacific Rim to Monterey Bay, California. Second only to chinooks in size, the workerlike chums usually return in two waves, summer and late fall when they are the last of the salmon to reach their home rivers. They leave their streams within months of spawning, and return with a territorial precision notable even among salmon after two to five years at sea.

Pinks, by comparison, are zoom salmon. After just a few months in freshwater and a single winter at sea, they return in great swarms of three- to six-pound fish. Throughout their range from the Sea of Japan to the Sacramento River, "humpies" spawn in alternating big and small years, and we know why. Because of their short life cycles, each year's pink salmon never mix with another's, so runs in odd- and even-numbered years have become genetically isolated and radically different in size.

Until 1992, steelhead were part of the *Salmo* tribe, but taxonomists reclassified the species as *O. mykiss.* They remain, however, the same object of passion for sports anglers, revered for their exuberance and, increasingly, for the difficulty of catching one on rod and reel. They are the only member of the *Oncorhynchus* tribe that spawns more than once.

Masu and amago occur only in Asian watersheds, and for most of our history with salmon have been considered a single species. Each has a close cousin that has not evolved an anadromous life cycle and remains exclusively in freshwater. They spend one or more years in their rivers, a winter in the ocean, and spawn in early fall after a full summer back in their rivers. In Japanese, these gold and silver salmon are *sakuramasu,* which means "cherry trout," because they return to the river at about the same time the cherry blossoms signal spring's arrival.

All Pacific salmon share common patterns of emergence, maturation, and reproduction that bind them to their streams and shape them for survival in the ocean. Chief among the survival mechanisms of the species is sheer abundance, since going the distance from egg to spawner is a numbers game. Ask anyone who's spent a summer on a counting tower. If S is the number of salmon that must return to perpetuate a healthy run, thousands of times S must be fertilized eggs. (My numbers are not scientific fact, but comparisons of magnitude that vary for each species.) Hundreds of times S must survive the delicate emergence into alevins, flashing bits of protein becoming living creatures in full view. These transparent, eyed beings hunker down in the substrate of their natal streams and feed off their own egg sacs during the still months of winter and early spring when predators are likely to leave them be. Then still hundreds of times S must survive to become fry, real fish with their egg sacs consumed, their bodies zipped up, fins, and tails. As juveniles or smolt, the new fish begin actively eating and being eaten. Herons, eagles, ospreys, and other birds thin their numbers as the salmon work their way downstream to the sea, and seals, gulls, ducks, otters, and bigger fish wait hungrily in the estuaries. And on most spawning rivers at the end of the twentieth century, the salmon are also decimated by pollution, dams, and the deadly, oxygen-poor reservoirs that have replaced swiftly flowing, highly oxygenated natural waters. Once in the sea, predators, including fishermen, claim their shares of the salmon runs, further reducing S until, finally, the survivors reach home to spawn.

◄ A bald eagle rips the flesh of a spawned-out chum salmon in the Alaska Chilkat Bald Eagle Preserve near Haines, Alaska.

LONG RANGE MIGRATIONS FASCINATE US. We are in awe of the distances salmon travel and their seemingly miraculous return to the exact point on earth where they emerged from their egg sacs to become fish. But salmon are of nature, and though our understanding of them remains incomplete, we know they do not require navigational miracles to reach home. Their in-stream and nearshore courses are probably set by a combination of rheotaxis—detection of the direction of flow—and their ability to sense temperature changes and combinations of smells from distinct watersheds. Their sense of smell is thousands of times more acute than that of dogs. A salmon can probably detect one part per trillion by smell, or, in martini equivalents, roughly one drop of vermouth in 500,000 barrels of gin.

At sea, during voyages that can be 10,000 miles long, the salmon do not aimlessly wander, nor do they leave the navigation to their prey by simply following their next meals. They clearly orient themselves in some way, and swim homeward with precision equaling electronically equipped ocean sailors. Celestial, solar, and sonar explanations for the salmon's ability to navigate have been explored and, generally, dismissed. Most recently, fish thinkers at the University of Washington—long a mecca for salmon science—proposed an electromagnetic solution to the puzzle of oceanic salmon migration. The earth's magnetic field produces an infinitely divided, arcing grid of extremely low-voltage currents, so a salmon or any other creature capable of detecting that voltage could track an arc on the grid that would lead it back to its starting point on the coast.

There, a salmon tunes its senses for local navigation by smell or rheotaxis to guide it to the patch of streambed or lake bottom from which it emerged many months earlier. Then, shocked by the freshwater of its birth, the beautiful swimmer transforms itself from a graceful silver voyager into a humpbacked reproductive aggressor, its bright ocean sheen replaced by the mottled combat of bruises to disguise itself in the shallows and present a fierce visage to competitors. The salmon passes a tower, a tallywhacker clicks, a biologist swats a mosquito, the journey ends, the journey begins.

THEN, SHOCKED BY THE FRESHWATER OF ITS BIRTH, THE BEAUTIFUL SWIMMER TRANSFORMS ITSELF FROM A GRACEFUL SILVER VOYAGER INTO A HUMPBACKED REPRODUCTIVE AGGRESSOR.

◄ *Of all the salmon species, the sockeye changes the most during spawning. Head of emerald green, body of red, humped back, and sharpened teeth—all are reminders that this creature is from an ancient time.*

THE WEB

Natalie Fobes

YOU CAN SMELL A SALMON STREAM a quarter mile away. The air is heavy with the sickly sweet scent of decaying salmon flesh, which clings like dew to the branches of the birches and willows along the path. As you get closer, the stench takes on a form of its own, shaped by river-beaten breezes, saturated and solid, in your face one second and gone the next. From this point on, you know you are not the only creature drawn to the river, as part of nature's web, to feast on the dying salmon.

57

THE SALMON WEAVES THROUGH the life stories of nature's creatures and

becomes the food, the sustenance, the life for fish, birds, mammals, and

man. And after the salmon dies, the threads of the web continue to be

spun, as the flesh breaks down into the basic nutrients needed by all life

to survive. In thousands of streams and bays around the Pacific Rim, the

salmon come no more. When the salmon disappear, the birds, bears,

orcas, and other creatures do too. And the web breaks.

PREVIOUS PAGES:

◄ ◄ ◄ *A brown bear tries in vain to snatch a leaping sockeye salmon on a river on the Alaska Peninsula. Because of the abundance of salmon and its rich, oily flesh, coastal brown bears can weigh up to 1,500 pounds.*

◄ ◄ *Normally bears catch salmon with their mouths, not their paws, at these falls on the Alaska Peninsula. Each bear defends its favorite fishing spot. Generally, the bigger the bear, the better the location.*

FACING PAGE:

◄ ◄ *Although many other salmon carcasses lie in the water, two bald eagles compete for a bit of fish on the bank. Each year over 3,000 bald eagles congregate on the Chilkat River near Haines, Alaska, to feast on chum salmon.*

◄ *Freshly fallen snow creates a backdrop for bald eagles on the Chilkat River.*

BARGING DOWN
THE RIVER

Salmon at the End of the Twentieth Century

BRAD MATSEN

THE BARGE FLEET OF THE CORPS OF ENGINEERS' Columbia River Juvenile Fish Transportation project is a confusing manifestation of hope. Like life-support machinery in an intensive-care ward, it is repulsive and fascinating at the same time, hard to look at, harder not to stare at once you do look. Every spring since 1972, on the south bank of the outwash pool at Lower Granite Dam, half the chinook, sockeye, and steelhead born in the upper Snake River begin life-saving but somehow pathetic barge rides to the sea. There, and downstream at Little Goose, Lower Monumental, and McNary dams, hustling crews wearing white hard hats load salmon in round-the-clock extravaganzas of concrete raceways, pumps, pipelines, and floodlights. At night, the scene is reminiscent of the techno-scape of the spaceship landing in *Close Encounters of the Third Kind,* remote, well-lit, organized, and urgent.

On each two-day trip aboard the gray and peach-colored steel barges, hundreds of thousands of young salmon hover in a netherworld of bubbling tanks, tended by a crew to net the few dead floaters and see to the diesels that run the aeration systems. Most of the salmon survive the trip downstream, and a sense of rescue abides in the workers, biologists, and bureaucrats. Without the barges, most of the salmon *would* perish in the turbines or reservoirs of the eight dams built and run by the Corps between Lower Granite and the free-flowing river at Bonneville. But less than a century ago, the young fish would have made the same trip with hundreds of millions of their kind in two or three weeks, transported by flowing water that is now a disorienting chain of lakes, concrete, and hubris.

The intricacies of a salmon's genetic code insist that it face upstream, into the current, and navigate to the sea tail first. Along the way, the signals, cues, and cautions of the river world are in rapids, falls, riffles, and eddies, each laden with distinct aromas and the nourishment of the riparian food web. A person aboard one of the barges on the same stretch of the Snake and Columbia rivers at the end of the twentieth century would note the entrances of dozens of substantial creeks—Penawawa, Deadman, Meadow, Glade, Alder, Sixprong, and Pine among them. The Palouse, Walla Walla, Umatilla, John Day, Deschutes, Klickitat, and Hood rivers make their more dramatic mergers from north and south into the great valleys, and the confluence of the Snake and the Columbia crackles with hydro-magic. Ashore, the

PREVIOUS PAGES:

◄◄ *A barge carrying salmon and steelhead smolts passes one of thirteen major dams that have turned the once-raging Columbia River into a series of flaccid reservoirs. Before the dams were built, salmon journeyed to the sea in as little as two to three weeks. Today it takes months and pushes at the limits of the biological time frame during which salmon are able to transform from freshwater to saltwater fish.*

◄ *On the banks of a stream near Stanley, Idaho, a biologist measures a wild chinook salmon smolt before entering the information into a computer. The study was designed to determine migration patterns of wild fish on the Snake and Columbia rivers.*

► *Millions of young fish are carried by barge around dams in an effort to increase the survival rate of chinook and steelhead fingerlings. Biologists estimate that as much as 30 percent of salmon smolts are killed by the dams, chewed up by turbines, or are victims of predation by birds and other fish.*

EVERY SPRING . . . HALF
THE CHINOOK, SOCKEYE,
AND STEELHEAD BORN IN
THE UPPER SNAKE RIVER
BEGIN . . . BARGE RIDES TO
THE SEA. . . . A SENSE OF
RESCUE ABIDES IN THE
WORKERS, BIOLOGISTS,
AND BUREAUCRATS.

LESS THAN A CENTURY AGO, THE YOUNG FISH WOULD HAVE MADE THE SAME TRIP WITH HUNDREDS OF MILLIONS OF THEIR KIND IN TWO OR THREE WEEKS, TRANSPORTED BY FLOWING WATER THAT IS NOW A DISORIENTING CHAIN OF LAKES, CONCRETE, AND HUBRIS.

river villages of Almota, Central Ferry, Riparia, Perry, Ayer, Matthew, Snake River, Humorist, Attalia, Wallula, Juniper, Plymouth, Alderdale, Moonax, Sundale, and Wishram—to name a few—appear and dissolve. And like giant creatures bent to drink, the cities of Pasco, Kennewick, Richland, Umatilla, and The Dalles loom and pass, the signatures of their smelters, granaries, paper plants, and mills remaining in clouds of smoke and steam. The basso rumblings of their engines sucking power from the river echo through the gorges and across the flats of the Columbia Plateau. The dams themselves are epic constructs, castle-like in their denial of scale until you are alongside, say, entering a navigation lock that raises or lowers a traveling barge a hundred feet or more from reservoir pool to outfall.

◄ David Samolik counts the smolts that died during the trip by barge. As with most salmon restoration efforts, the multimillion-dollar barging program is controversial. Proponents claim it increases the survival chances for young salmon. But many tribes and biologists say that rather than helping the runs, the confining conditions on the barges may actually hurt the juvenile salmon by increasing the risk of disease.

MERIWETHER LEWIS AND WILLIAM CLARK would have a hard time imagining the Snake and Columbia just two centuries after they crested the Great Divide and worked their way down the Pacific slope in 1804. "The multitudes of this fish are almost inconceivable," Clark wrote of salmon, after the autumn of his arrival in the Northwest Territory. Of course, the place was perfect for salmon, the salmon perfect for the place, and, for better or worse, both were perfect for human beings. Then, the undammed Columbia and its tributaries offered 12,935 miles of pristine habitat to 15 to 20 million salmon, weaving them into a watershed that drains a quarter of a million square miles. About 70,000 people, including many whose ancestors had been in those environs for thousands of years, lived in the Snake and Columbia basins by the middle decades of the nineteenth century, the last years of the natural river. According to new archaeological evidence, human settlement far distant from modern tribes began along the rivers about 14,000 years ago.

In 1994, more than 6 million people are crowded against the life force of the Columbia and Snake rivers. We have traded the ancient, free-running spawning habitat for 7.6 million acres of irrigated farmland, cheap timber, and the power from 136 dams to drive commerce and development. To the newborn nation of the United States of America, dams were part of the vision of paradise. Engineers were priests, and the forces of nature mere puzzles with certain solutions. Habitat destruction to encourage commerce is not an aberration of industrial culture but a definitive characteristic, and no nation can claim restraint on behalf of salmon. Even today, as the somber notes of acute ecosystem crisis are sounding in the Sacramento, Columbia, Fraser, and dozens of other North American watersheds, politicians support destructive logging and mining practices in Alaska and British Columbia, assuring us that they will not harm their healthy salmon runs.

WHETHER MOTIVATED BY LONG-RANGE VISION or short-term greed, the people of the Pacific Northwest and an entire continent tacitly agree to the bargain that is killing off salmon. Millions of other people in Asia and Europe have agreed to similar alterations in their relationships with the habitat of Pacific and Atlantic salmon. The mainland drainages of the Tumen, Amur, Anadyr, Markova, Elbe, Danube, Rhine, Thames, Spey, Hudson, and Connecticut rivers and the numberless shorter watercourses of the Newfoundland, Kuril, and Japanese archipelagoes once bloomed with salmon every year. Even though the runs have almost vanished from many rivers, bright salmon are favored by people living nearer the ocean, and dark, upriver fish by inland folks. Salmon haven't spawned near Zurich for generations, but people there still like to eat colored-up, late-season salmon, as though by genetic memory, and some brokers specialize in selling them similar fish from other rivers with surviving runs.

Salmon have been food for as long as other critters have been around to eat them, and our myths, ceremonies, and respect have been engendered as much by gratitude for a meal as by appreciation for their enigmatic spirits. The earliest treaties, agreements, and

---

HABITAT DESTRUCTION TO ENCOURAGE COMMERCE IS NOT AN ABERRATION OF INDUSTRIAL CULTURE BUT A DEFINITIVE CHARACTERISTIC, AND NO NATION CAN CLAIM RESTRAINT ON BEHALF OF SALMON.

▶ *Clear-cutting of forests like this one on Vancouver Island in British Columbia, Canada, destroys salmon streams. Vegetation that shades the stream has been stripped, raising the water temperature, said biologist Kelly Wilcox after he finished taking a reading. The stream is now too warm for salmon. He added that the bare hillsides will likely erode with the winter rains and cover the spawning gravel needed by salmon.*

conciliations among the people of the Pacific Rim sorted out rights to salmon, first as matters of tradition, then as matters of law, but always because salmon are vital as food. For thousands of years in the human relationship with salmon, though, nobody trapped, caught, or ate anything anonymously. The links between water, fish, trees, and people were not scientifically defined, but they were perfectly clear and understood in myths and traditions. Commerce in distant markets and cash economies broke those instinctive bonds forever and replaced them with the impersonal networks of industrial fishing, canning, and freezing. Now, salmon reach tables around the world but carry no ecological return address.

Putting up Pacific salmon on an industrial scale began in 1864 on the Sacramento River when the Hume brothers—William, George, Robert, and Joseph—arrived with a tinsmith, Andrew Hapgood. Sixty years before they came into the territory, Nicolas Appert, a vintner, brewer, and chef, had invented the canning process and won Napoleon Bonaparte's 1,200-franc prize for coming up with a way to feed advancing armies. Subsequent refinements in the process eliminated some of the spoilage that plagued canners and armies, tin cans replaced glass jars, and, finally, Pasteur tied bacteria to disease. Not incidentally, he figured out why food rotted and what to do about it. In 1840, the first canned salmon in North America was packed on the Bay of Fundy, not too far north of Maine, the childhood home of the Humes and Hapgood.

At first, the packers cut out their cans with tinsnips, soldered them by hand, filled each with the very tasty, very expensive salmon that was worth about one dollar a can in England, crimped and soldered tops, and submitted the miraculous package to heat in a retort. A good tinsmith could make 100 cans a day, and an entire year's pack was less than 100,000 cans. Trapping the salmon in the river was easy and cheap, so in short order, Hapgood and the Humes got rich and expanded into real canneries from their family shed on the river.

In a few years, a combination of salmon lust on the Sacramento and dredging and hydrologic

COMMERCE IN DISTANT MARKETS AND CASH ECONOMIES BROKE THOSE INSTINCTIVE BONDS FOREVER AND REPLACED THEM WITH THE IMPERSONAL NETWORKS OF INDUSTRIAL FISHING, CANNING, AND FREEZING.

◄ *To walk into a fish plant in Russia is to step back in time. For ten hours a day, women stand in hip-deep pits to gut and clean salmon on wood counters that are scarred and pocked with the knife-marks of a generation. Much of the salmon is canned or salted and sent to Moscow.*

► Literally turned upside down, the Yankee Fork of Idaho's Salmon River still bears the scars of a gold dredge which half a century ago destroyed five miles of stream in five years. Historically, Idaho streams produced 45 percent of the Snake and Columbia river runs. Today it is less than 10 percent.

mining, a particularly virulent method that blasts enormous quantities of mud and gravel into the rivers and streams, had just about wiped out the runs and spawning beds in that watershed. So the salmon canners spread north, first to the Rogue River, then the Columbia, the Fraser, and the smaller watercourses in between. Competitors challenged the Humes and Hapgood, and eventually, fleets of square-riggers sailed for Alaskan waters. As the years ticked over into the "American Century," the unbridled canners were packing salmon on every spawning river from California to the Arctic Circle, and canned salmon began its eighty-year run as a staple food. From 1870 to 1950, you could open ten cupboards any-where in Europe or North America and probably find a can of salmon in seven of them. Markets for salmon that would keep for more than a week seemed endless and the rush was on, every bit the equal of gold fever.

Though salmon traps and weirs were the mainstays of hundreds of chugging canneries, eventually men in boats had to venture away from the rivers into the sea to supply the pack-ing lines. What we now celebrate as commercial salmon fishing had arrived on the Pacific. Every spring, full-rigged ships sailed north from San Francisco, across the Gulf of Alaska, west along the Aleutians, through Unimak Pass, and into the Bering Sea. The Alaska fleet was the last hurrah for the square-riggers, including *Star of India, Abner Coburn, Benjamin F. Packard,* and *Glory of the Seas.* In Bristol Bay, the ships would anchor off any one of the wildly rich salmon rivers like the Egegik, Naknek, and Nushagak. Laborers would haul lumber, nets, cans, and dories to the beach, and build or repair the cannery. The ship captain became the superintendent ashore, the fishermen fished until the ship was full, and, with luck, made the return trip. Fishermen were a cut above the cannery laborers in the chain of the enterprise because they shared in the profits depending on how many salmon they caught. Not until the 1920s, when many of the once vigorous runs of Bristol Bay and elsewhere became pathetic trickles, did anyone give much thought to restraint.

DREDGING AND HYDROLOGIC MINING, A PARTICULARLY VIRULENT METHOD THAT BLASTS ENORMOUS QUANTITIES OF MUD AND GRAVEL INTO THE RIVERS AND STREAMS . . . WIPE OUT RUNS AND SPAWNING BEDS.

◂ ◂ Despite gale-force winds, fishermen Jim Schmidt and Pete Blackwell haul in their gill net. With three weeks to make or break the season, fishermen in Bristol Bay, Alaska, work in all kinds of weather and often twenty-four hours a day.
◂ Gunwale to gunwale and net to net, gill-net fishermen compete for fish on the south line of the Egegik fishing district in Bristol Bay, Alaska.

Almost everybody agrees that traps, wheels, and weirs are by far the most efficient and, if properly controlled, sustainable methods for catching salmon. When you can be sure the fish you kill to eat are from a specific stream, you can let enough through your weir or trap to guarantee the health of the run before you take any for food. Tightly managed traps and stream barriers are still common on the nearshore Asian runs, while industrial-scale Japanese, Korean, and Russian fleets fish offshore, mainly on chinook, sockeye, and chum. Hardy, independent fishermen have dominated the North American fisheries since the '20s, bearing the same names as their boats—seiners, gillnetters, and trollers. Seining spread to the Pacific with Austrian and Croatian immigrants, gillnetting with Scandinavians, and

SEINERS FISH WITH GREAT ENCIRCLING NETS... GILLNETTERS ENSNARE THE SALMON IN A NEARLY INVISIBLE WEB... TROLLERS USE SIMPLE HOOKS AND LINES THAT MAKE THEM, MANY PEOPLE SUGGEST, ARTISTS AMONG CRAFTSMEN.

◄ ◄ *With graceful motions, troller Kirk Wollin hauls in a coho salmon from the ocean near Sitka, Alaska.*
◄ *The white corks of a seiner's set bob on the surface of Puget Sound in Washington state.*

trolling with the Portuguese and Italians of Monterey Bay, California. Different kinds of fishermen are clannish in their opinions of each other, but they are celebrated equally in songs, poems, magazines, books, and are all worthy of legend. Some die at sea, some get rich, some just have a good time. Seiners fish with great encircling nets, gillnetters with nets that hang vertically, ensnaring the salmon in a nearly invisible web, and trollers with the simple hooks and lines that make them, many people suggest, artists among craftsmen.

Catching and selling salmon is critical to the commercial proposition, but the idyll is found elsewhere. Pioneer trollers from California to Alaska, for instance, made their lures by hand on harbor days when the sea was too rough to fish. Anchored in timbered coves or tied to docks in Moss Landing, Neah Bay, Campbell River, and Sitka, they snipped rough shapes from sheets of brass and copper, placed the metal over hollows carved in ironbark, and, with ball peen hammers, tapped in subtle curves until hunch and experience told them to stop. The spoons they made imitated schooling pelagics—herring, candlefish, and capelin—the prey of king salmon, in turn the prey of the fishermen. Old-time trollers say that during breaks in the wind which kept them off the grounds you could hear the *tink, tink, tink* of hammers hanging in the air, mingling with the dense, sticky aromas of the forests and fish ports. Who wouldn't have gone fishing?

Almost all commercial salmon fleets fish some distance away from the spawning streams, and therein lies the soul of international salmon politics. Because salmon are migratory and anadromous, they pass through many governmental jurisdictions, each of which seeks to control them for reasons of profit or conservation. Nations, states, and the people whose ancestors predate the Northern European version of civilization claim them. Salmon, of course, carry no passports and belong to no one.

Until the middle of the century, the hegemony of the canned salmon industry dominated governments, treaties, and management. Nobody was going to buck the tide of profits that swelled from the sea every summer, buoying the economies of the Pacific Northwest, British Columbia, and Alaska. (The salmon fisheries of Asia remained, for the most part, artisanal or subsistence through most of the history of the industrial North American fleets.) Prewar treaties virtually ignored tribal claims, but did provide the framework for ongoing negotiations, most critically between the United States and Canada. Salmon from the Fraser drainage wend their way through the waters off Alaska and Washington as well as British Columbia on their way home, and Columbia River salmon, most notably chinooks and coho, brush both sides of Vancouver Island. Each government has something to gain and something to lose in acknowledging the other's right to catch and manage those fish.

NOBODY WAS GOING TO BUCK THE TIDE OF PROFITS THAT SWELLED FROM THE SEA EVERY SUMMER, BUOYING THE ECONOMIES OF THE PACIFIC NORTHWEST, BRITISH COLUMBIA, AND ALASKA.

▶ *A fisherman holds $21,000 he made for nine days' work in 1988. Big bucks can be made—and lost—during a season in Bristol Bay, Alaska. But fishing is risky and many hold second jobs to make ends meet.*

FOLLOWING THE GREAT WAR IN THE PACIFIC, the recovering Asian nations of Korea, Japan, China, and the Soviet Union brought new complexity to commercial salmon diplomacy. As the victors, the United States, Canada, and the Soviet Union dictated postwar terms for fishing on the high seas in a series of agreements that established the International North Pacific Fisheries Commission. Because most North American salmon mingle with Asian stocks in the fertile latitudes of the Pacific gyre, the several nations agreed to create a permanent forum to establish and alter rights to fish on the high seas. The treaties and agreements of the 1950s encouraged the first international scientific inquiry into the health of Pacific salmon, and were a prelude to the vigorous global markets that now drive the commercial fisheries. They did not, however, address the fishing rights of the descendants of the early salmon people.

Resource rights in the Canadian and American cultures are, by and large, land-based. When, instead of guns, alcohol, and disease, the time for negotiations and reparations reached the frontier, the European conquerors overlooked fishing rights. The earliest settlements addressed land ownership, and references to salmon were oblique or absent. In the 1960s, however, that apparent injustice began to rise to the forefront of the American and Canadian civil rights and Native claims movements. In Washington state, a federal judge awarded the Native American tribes of the Pacific Northwest fully half of all salmon taken commercially, plus fish for subsistence and ceremonial purposes. The decision, by a judge named George Boldt, was a landmark, and led to similar claims and decisions in British Columbia and elsewhere. Alaska Natives, however, had already settled for land and permits to fish, which they can sell, if they choose, for cash. In Alaska, subsistence fishing by all citizens was also granted the highest priority in the order of salmon harvest, followed by commercial and then sport fishing.

Perhaps more than any single force, the passion of angling has fueled the modern salmon conservation and habitat recovery movements on the Pacific. Some people believe that killing or hurting any animal, even a fish, for fun is patently immoral. But sport fishing is deeply wound into the European and North American cultures. The appeal of catching a salmon, say a big chinook, on a rod and reel is a soul-altering experience, and those who do it routinely never seem to weary of the act. And because sport fishing cuts across all layers in the social, political, and power strata, votes, lobbying, and public relations on behalf of salmon lately carry as much voltage as the canning industry did fifty years ago. Sports anglers are in fact customers of a multibillion-dollar industry every bit the equal of the old packing empires, but based on rods, reels, boats, motors, beer, baseball hats, and airline tickets instead of cases of 48-tall cans.

The town of Campbell River, on Vancouver Island in British Columbia, declares itself the Salmon Fishing Capital of the World for five months a year. Tens of thousands of true believers from around the globe converge to numb the otherwise quiet coastal village with hordes of cars, campers, and boat trailers. Daily flotillas of as many as 1,000 outboard skiffs, cabin boats, and substantial yachts surround the dominant headland, Cape Mudge, which marks the northern end of the Strait of Georgia. The sporting fleet is a pesky hazard, noted in the log of every fishing boat, cruise ship, ferry, and steamer en route through the Inside Passage to Southeast Alaska.

The homeward-bound salmon, too, are pinched into the gap at Campbell River, and are sometimes so thick you can't drop a line to the bottom without catching one. The prize is a big chinook, or "spring" in the local idiom, many of which top fifty pounds. Some anglers troll for them, some cast, some even use flies, but mooching is the technique favored by locals, who use a whippy eleven- or twelve-foot rod, a single-action reel, a long, fine leader, and a live or cut herring. The strike of a big fish while mooching can feel like a bounce on the

bottom or like an assault, you just never know. But once you're hooked up, a half hour or more of arm-shredding work comes next. Guides show even the greenest tourists what to do, other locals will smoke and ship the fish, lodges offer food and beds. Sport fishing is big business.

Campbell River was also the home of Roderick Haig-Brown, one of angling's most celebrated conservationists and writers. He died in 1976, but was once the magistrate of the town and the author of *Return to the River* and many other books about the grace, truths, and meditations to be found in fishing. He lived and raised his family with his wife, Mary, in a cabin he called "Above Tide," a quarter-mile from the mouth of the short river from which the village takes its name. At tidewater, the Campbell flows into the Tyee Pool, known for big salmon and an exclusive club. The pool has drawn celebrities and the most passionate of anglers seeking to qualify for membership limited to those who have caught spring salmon weighing over thirty pounds while fishing with artificial lures from a rowboat. Just north of the Tyee Pool, the biggest pulp mill in central British Columbia steams and roars day and night, fed by timber cut under liberal harvest rules that have destroyed countless miles of salmon habitat. The springs in the Tyee Pool, of course, are smaller and fewer as the years go by.

In 1961, Haig-Brown published *The Living Land,* a commissioned work for the British Columbia Natural Resources Conference, in which he wrote:

> It is hoped that the book will serve to advance the cause and philosophy of conservation among the peoples of the world. "Immense natural resources"—"vast natural wealth"—"inexhaustable natural resources"—these phrases and many others like them have been used about practically every geographic and political division in North America. They have long been the treasured toys of promoters and boomers and boosters, the happy playthings of politicians, the sad and doubtful comfort of struggling settlers and ordinary working people.
>
> A conservationist fights many battles, varying in scale all the way from the

PERHAPS MORE THAN ANY SINGLE FORCE, THE PASSION OF ANGLING HAS FUELED THE MODERN SALMON CONSERVATION AND HABITAT RECOVERY MOVEMENTS ON THE PACIFIC.

◄ *The days are over—at least temporarily—when the catch of the day hangs outside a sport fishing guide service in the coastal community of Ilwaco, Washington. With fewer fish returning to the rivers, the ocean seasons have grown shorter and, in 1994, were banned for the year off the coast of Washington, Oregon, and California.*

attempted protection of some individual species of wildlife to the supreme issue of proper use of soil, air, and water; and every fight is complicated, if not forced, by the false urgency and outdated sanctity of progress. . . . Timber, soil, fisheries, oil and minerals, even water power, become more, not less valuable with delay.

🐟

CONSERVATION BECAME INSTINCTIVE to the early people who fished familiar runs and who viscerally understood the link between the health of the fish and their own survival. The ancient salmon people suffered terribly and immediately when their overfishing brought famine and death, and the deadly consequences of resource abuse were also more quickly apparent among their smaller populations. If they took too many salmon, they died; if modern people take too many salmon, we order the pork chops. When Lewis and Clark got their first look at Pacific salmon at the beginning of the nineteenth century, barely a billion people were aboard the home planet; by 1945, the population had swelled to 2.5 billion; in 1994, to about 5.5 billion; and by 2020, we will number 11 billion. We have moved away from our early, more instinctive relationship with our food, but we have not succeeded in forming a new paradigm for mutual survival on our increasingly crowded, hungry earth.

Our first stab at creating a new ecological partnership with salmon was simply to grow more of them and we quickly figured out how to do it. Some of the migrating fry and fingerlings that ride those Snake and Columbia barges hatched in the natural gravel of creeks, as their ancestors have for thousands of years, but far more of them flickered into life in the plastic racks of hatcheries. Fish culture is ancient in its beginnings, dating back at least 2,000 years to the Roman Empire in Europe, and 4,000 years in Asia. Our collective impulse to domesticate land, birds, cattle, sheep, and other animals seems to be among the most

"A CONSERVATIONIST FIGHTS MANY BATTLES, VARYING IN SCALE ALL THE WAY FROM THE ATTEMPTED PROTECTION OF SOME INDIVIDUAL SPECIES OF WILDLIFE TO THE SUPREME ISSUE OF PROPER USE OF SOIL, AIR, AND WATER."

◄ *The stillness of a sleepy Sunday in 1986 was shattered when more than 2,500 salmon leapt from the water and died on the banks of Seattle's Duwamish River. Biologists believe toxic chemicals in the water killed the fish.*

powerful in human nature, so it's no wonder we responded to disappearing salmon with hatcheries. The good news is that it worked for awhile; the bad news is that nature bats last.

The Americans built their first hatchery for Pacific salmon in 1872 on the McCloud River in California; the first in Canada was on the Fraser at Bon Accord, near what is now a suburb of Vancouver. Early on, the North Americans focused on chinooks, and even tried using them to restock depleted runs of Atlantic salmon on the East Coast. That didn't work, of course, and they learned that *Salmo* and *Oncorhynchus* were of different species. Japan imported modern salmon hatchery methods and technology from the United States and Canada in 1889. Soon after, chinook eggs from Pacific Northwest hatcheries were shipped as far away as Australia and New Zealand, where they took hold. Hatcheries for egg production and enhancement of natural runs were so successful that the dam builders counted on them to heal the rivers. In the 1930s, when Grand Coulee Dam destroyed every inch of spawning habitat in 1,000 miles of the entire upper Columbia, people wrote songs about building dams, building fish, and our dominion over nature.

Hatcheries remained largely the business of government fish-growing and dam-building agencies until the 1970s, when Alaskans voted to allow what they called "private, non-profit hatcheries." Most people refer to this kind of salmon-making as "ranching." You hatch the fish in controlled conditions with far greater than natural survival rates, turn them out to pasture— the ocean—and wait for their return the next summer or in two, three, or four years. The idea was to transform the annual variations of some of the runs into dependable—domesticated?— runs. The salmon pass through the open waters to give commercial and sports fleets the first shot at them (and, not incidentally, gain political and financial support for the hatcheries), and then you harvest the rest at the hatchery to meet expenses and take eggs for the next crop.

That was the plan, but a few bold scientists at the University of Alaska and elsewhere are starting to suspect the high expectations for salmon ranching will fall to the truth in an old

OUR COLLECTIVE IMPULSE TO DOMESTICATE LAND, BIRDS, CATTLE, SHEEP, AND OTHER ANIMALS SEEMS TO BE AMONG THE MOST POWERFUL IN HUMAN NATURE, SO IT'S NO WONDER WE RESPONDED TO DISAPPEARING SALMON WITH HATCHERIES.

▶ *Thousands of chinook salmon race to the surface of their net pen to feast on food pellets thrown by a worker. With wild runs under assault, private and public hatcheries and farms are raising millions of salmon each year, much to the concern of many biologists and environmentalists.*

BECAUSE EARLY LIFE IN A
HATCHERY IS EASY LIVING
FOR A SALMON, ALL THOSE
SURVIVAL TRAITS—
POWERFUL PHYSIOLOGY
AND ANCIENT INSTINCTS—
ARE NOT FULLY SELECTED
AND TESTED. HATCHERY
SALMON ARE WEAKER
SALMON.

▲ *Many British Columbia salmon farms raise their own smolts in hatcheries like this one near Sechelt, British Columbia. Brian Lymer covers the trays to prevent predation by gulls.*

adage: *Nullum gratuitum prandium*—"there is no free lunch." Regardless of their origins, salmon compete for food in rivers, bays, and oceans, and in 1993, only fragments of the expected runs of both wild and ranch pink salmon returned to Prince William Sound, home of the world's biggest hatcheries and, in 1989, site of America's worst oil spill from the *EXXON Valdez*. Wild salmon also can interbreed with hatchery fish, which may reduce their ability to survive. If a female hatchery pink salmon spawns with a wild male pink salmon, for instance, succeeding generations of that union will inherit only part of the precious genetic code of the wild. Because early life in a hatchery is easy living for a salmon, survival traits—powerful physiology and ancient instincts—are not fully selected and tested. Hatchery salmon are weaker salmon.

At about the time the success of hatcheries and ocean ranches peaked in the mid-1970s, a professor at the University of Washington was refining the tools and methods for the next step in the direction of domestication: salmon farming. While hatcheries released salmon into the pasture of the sea, farming would maintain them in captivity from birth to dinner table, like chickens or beeves. Loren Donaldson figured out how to rear trout and Atlantic salmon in captivity, and Norway, the most salmon-desperate nation in the world, snapped to attention.

THE EUROPEANS HAD LONG SINCE OVERFISHED and overpopulated their watersheds, and Norway had battalions of out-of-work fishermen sitting at the dock. With Donaldson's breakthroughs, they saw a way to put everybody back to work. Marine trout and salmon farms were controlled by local banks, their boards of directors had to include fishermen, and the Norwegian government began an aggressive marketing campaign. By 1980, world production of farmed salmon was a modest 25,000 tons, out of a total salmon pack of about 700,000 tons. By 1993, the Norwegians had been joined in force by Canadian, Irish, Chilean, Japanese, Russian, American, and New Zealand farmers and were producing about 250,000 tons each year out of total world production of about 800,000 tons.

The farms, too, have proved to be far from foolproof. The industry has almost collapsed more than once when a disease or a plankton bloom that kills salmon but doesn't hurt human consumers kills the fish in all the pens along an entire coast. Tons of salmon end up on the market at the same time, the glut drives down the price, and everybody loses money. Commercial fishermen loathe the farms because they compete directly with the wild or hatchery salmon they catch and sell. More profoundly, farmed salmon seem so terribly unnatural to those fishermen and other people whose lives are entwined with the wild fish. And people who eat wild salmon regularly know from the first bite whether they've been served a slab of farmed salmon in a restaurant that does not own up to the fact. The taste is definitely more bland, the flesh not as firm, the color often a pale imitation of the redder wild salmon. On the waterfronts of the Northwest Coast, fishermen's pickup trucks sport bumper stickers that declare "real salmon don't eat pellets," a reference to the universal

farmed salmon food called the Oregon Moist Pellet, a protein-fiber morsel akin to chicken feed.

Without a doubt, our hungry world will raise protein for food, but farmed salmon are a bad bet even if they don't place wild salmon at risk. Aquaculturists think tilapia (an African lake fish), catfish, and shrimp will be the protein staples of the twenty-first century because they grow fast and are far less susceptible to disease than salmon. To keep salmon on our plates, most of the wiser food gurus and ecologists are urging restoration of natural runs, habitat rehabilitation, and restraints on commercial production. In fifty years, we will surely remember as prideful our attempts to mend the shredded eco-fabric of a watershed like the Columbia River. Hatchery midwifery, farms, and fingerlings barged around dams have only postponed the disastrous consequences of our collision with Pacific salmon. We reckoned, incorrectly, that we could disturb elegant cosmic rhythms and make them right with our brains and muscle. We were wrong. Salmon are not vegetables with eyes.

AFTER 100 YEARS OF STEADY PROFITS and memorable strikes on rod and reel, though, the silver messengers of the *Oncorhynchus* tribe are finally inspiring wisdom among many of us whose lives they have enriched. The extinction of a run of salmon somehow weakens us unnaturally, that much is clear, whether we understand the details or not. We sense the same panic and passion that rose in us when we stood a death watch over Martha, the very last passenger pigeon on earth. She died on September 1, 1914, in the Cincinnati zoo, after a commercial hunting orgy had obliterated her species for eternity, and her passing made the front pages of just about every paper in America. People wept openly. Now, Martha is stuffed and perched on a branch in a glass case in the Smithsonian Institution, reminding us that extinction for profit and commerce is a dreadful by-product of our civilization. A lot of us feel the same sense of bitter dread about salmon.

BUMPER STICKERS DECLARE "REAL SALMON DON'T EAT PELLETS," A REFERENCE TO THE UNIVERSAL FARMED SALMON FOOD CALLED THE OREGON MOIST PELLET, A PROTEIN-FIBER MORSEL AKIN TO CHICKEN FEED.

◄ *At sunset, a worker feeds salmon reared in net pens. Salmon farming is labor intensive, and caring for the fish is a twenty-four-hour-a-day job.*

Lonesome Larry, a sockeye that probably rode one of those barges from Lower Granite, now reposes, mounted, in the office of the governor of Idaho. In the hands of a fisheries biologist, Larry gave his milt to fertilize the last female eggs of his species, and then died. He was born in Redfish Lake, joined by a tributary to the Snake, then to the Columbia, then to the Pacific Ocean by waters now otherwise occupied. In 1992, the federal fisheries agency declared Larry and the handful of other surviving Redfish sockeye to be endangered, and placed the run under care as wards of the people of the United States and the world. They declared other Columbia River runs to be threatened, also requiring special protection.

By law, the governments of the United States, Washington, Oregon, Idaho, and Alaska and, by treaty, British Columbia, Japan, and Russia, must all pay special attention to the spawn of Lonesome Larry. Biologists will hatch and rear his offspring in captivity until enough of them are around to risk a trip downstream. The Bonneville Power Authority, Corps of Engineers, Bureau of Reclamation, and the owners of other dams in the watershed are also supposed to be cooperating to save Larry and his kin. Instead, the smelting companies, which consume 47 percent of the power from the eight Corps of Engineers' dams, are buying television and radio time to tell us that without aluminum we can't have airplanes and trips to visit loved ones and sick friends. Development boosters are reminding us that our society made a choice on the Columbia and Snake, it cost us the salmon, and jobs are more important than fish. Anglers and commercial fishermen are still laying claim to "their" salmon, government agencies are defending their budgets and hatcheries, and agribusinesses their irrigation networks. Albert Einstein noted that we are fools to try to solve big problems with the same kind of thinking that made them. So it is with Pacific salmon.

"When you have a system that is so altered from its natural state, it's hard to know what to do for the salmon," said one of the biologists who works on the Columbia barges that, ultimately, are not saving the salmon. "Maybe nothing. But I really can't stand that. I just can't."

"WHEN YOU HAVE A SYSTEM THAT IS SO ALTERED FROM ITS NATURAL STATE, IT'S HARD TO KNOW WHAT TO DO FOR THE SALMON."

▶ *Endangered Snake River sockeye salmon swim in a pen at a hatchery near Boise, Idaho.*

COMMERCE

Natalie Fobes

ABOUT THE TIME THE SNOW DISAPPEARS for the last time in May, the first of the sockeye salmon begin their journey home to the rivers and streams of Bristol Bay, Alaska. Just as the red salmon return each spring, so do the men and women of the Bristol Bay fishery. Doctors, lawyers, drug runners, teachers, writers and chemists, biologists and psychologists all leave their jobs Outside and join the locals to chase the gold that rides on the backs of the reds.

PREVIOUS PAGES:

◄ ◄ *Loaded to the gunwales, a thirty-two-foot gillnetter races to off-load its salmon. Bristol Bay boasts the largest salmon run in the world, with 44 to 66 million fish returning within a three-week period. But fishing openings are limited. Every minute a net is out of the water means fish that can't be caught and money that won't be made.*

◄ *Crewmen haul in a net by hand during a heavy fishing period in Bristol Bay.*

◄ *Days are long on the Alaskan fishing grounds and move steadily through the nights with little pause. For the people who work the "slime line"—often college students looking for adventure—hours are filled with lots of salmon guts and little sleep. During a good season they may make their tuition for the coming school year. During many seasons they leave with little more than the money in their pockets.*

▼ *"You can sleep in the winter" is a saying often repeated during the season. Fishermen like Tim DeLapp grab a few minutes of rest whenever they can.*

► *And when the nights finally darken in July, and most of the fish are already in the rivers, Brad Larsen and Jim Schmit catch up on their cribbage.*

◀ *During the height of the Alaska summer, the sun rarely dips far below the horizon. Kelly Kerrone and Dale Gorman take a break to enjoy the northern-latitude experience of watching a simultaneously setting and rising sun.*
▶ *Carrying on a long-time fishing tradition, Pete Blackwell kisses the first salmon of the season before tossing it back in the water. Old-timers claim that this will bring good luck—and good fish—during the fishing season.*

SOME ARE IN IT for the money. Others, the legacy fishermen, the sons and daughters of the men and women who started fishing when it was a good way of life, say it's the only life they know— or want. For the season their life's reality is cramming into a boat's cabin the size of a pickup truck cab, fishing for thirty-six hours at a stretch and sleeping for three, carrying thousands of dollars in their black-nailed hands, blasting their engines to life and running with the wind at their faces and the seas at their feet, wrestling with nature, trying to outguess her, outsmart her, beat her, embrace her.

THROUGH FOG TONED IN SEPIA SHADES, I walked past rusting boats and

battered buildings and stopped on the bank of a Russian river. In front of

me a man rowed his homemade skiff across the water. Behind him were

rows of boathouses on piers, bent with the years like old men's knees.

Beside me the inevitable fishing-port cat stared with eyes wide with hope

and belly tight to bone. I knew this fishing village of Poronaysk on

Sakhalin Island was a very long way from home. It seemed I had stepped

back in time to the years before World War I, before widespread use of

stainless steel tables, modern canning lines, and hydraulically controlled

booms. Today, as then, the Russians fish with set-net traps in bays and rivers.

PREVIOUS PAGES:

◀ ◀ *Oil coats the surface of a river near the port of Poronaysk, Russia.*
◀ *One of the new breed of entrepreneurs, this private fisherman is a professor in Moscow during the winter months. As the Russian economy opens up, the government has allowed limited private fishing by small companies.*

◀ *Like his father before him, a Russian fisherman takes time out for a cigarette while off-loading salmon.*
▶ *Four times a day during the peak of the season, Russian fishermen row to a set-net trap full of salmon near Sakhalin Island to clear it.*

◄ *Using a stick to lift the corner of a set net, a Russian fisherman judges how many fish have been trapped. During the peak of the season, a set net may yield more than ten tons of salmon at a time.*

▲ *While much of Russia's salmon is canned, some is salted and stored in barrels of brine. Since most of the fish is shipped to Moscow, it is difficult to find salmon in the Far East. At one store in the heart of the salmon region, a limited number of cans went on sale for four hours only, once a week.*

► *Struggling against the weight of the set net, fishermen haul salmon onto the fishing boat.*

◄ *A swimmer tries to catch one of the thousands of salmon that surround him. The Ochepukha River's 1989 return on Russia's Sakhalin Island was the second greatest in history.*

▲ *With hands red and raw, Russian workers take a break to smoke, relax, and gossip at the Druzhba collective in Poronaysk, Sakhalin Island. The women are paid according to how much fish their team processes per shift.*

©Natalie Fobes/National Geographic Society

▲ ▶ *Shyly clutching her doll, a young girl stares at the first Americans she has ever seen in the fishing community of Poronaysk.*

▶ *With ten hours of cutting fish behind her, a Russian cannery worker takes a moment to freshen up before going home.*

EVERYTHING I NEEDED TO KNOW about Japan's culture of salmon I learned

at 4:30 one chilled October morning when I left behind the sleeping

silence of predawn Tokyo and slipped inside a side door at Tsukiji Fish

Market. Horns blared, engines roared, workers shouted. Stacked on tables

and benches were thousands of species of sea life—fish in boxes, fish in

bins, fish in aquariums and saltwater tanks and freshwater buckets.

A room the size of a football field held table after table of salmon.

I had memorized all the Japanese fishing facts years ago and had traded them like baseball cards with other fishery groupies. But those facts became real when I saw the market's fifty-seven acres crammed with samples of the day's offerings. Japan fishes in every ocean on earth. The Japanese eat seventy-five pounds of seafood per person per year. Japan's hatcheries produce 38 percent of the world's salmon. Japanese companies own 80 percent of North American salmon processors and buy 90 percent of Alaska's salmon. Japan is the center of the salmon world.

BRITISH COLUMBIA'S SUNSHINE COAST is home to scores of farms nestled in bays at the foot of fir- and cedar-cloaked mountains. It was only a matter of time before entrepreneurs tried to raise salmon in nets. Grow the salmon in saltwater net pens and harvest them when the market demands, they said. It just makes sense. No longer would the supply be tied to the fishing seasons, with prices dictated by fishermen. The Norwegians have been doing it for years with their Atlantic salmon, they said. Farming might even save the wild salmon, they said, because fishermen wouldn't have to catch so many fish. To hear these people talk, salmon farming was going to save the salmon world.

And so in the '80s scores of farms popped up along the Sunshine Coast near Sechelt, B.C. Depending on whom you talked to, salmon farming was either an economic savior to the communities of out-of-work loggers and fishermen or the devil come back to destroy the environment and the wild salmon.

The boom went bust. The algae blooms were particularly bad for a couple years straight. In the wild, salmon can avoid the gill-choking water, but trapped in a 100-foot-by-100-foot net pen they cannot. Many of the companies overspent. Most found that raising salmon cost a whole lot more than they thought. And with cheaper priced coho salmon flooding the market from Chilean salmon farms, they couldn't make enough money to pay their expenses. Many farms went into receivership.

PREVIOUS PAGES:

◄◄ *The sunlight filtered through the waters of British Columbia's Sunshine Coast, its emerald color indicating another algae bloom was under way. I lay eighty-five feet below the surface and watched 57,000 chinook salmon swim round and round the perimeter of the farm's net pen. This was just one of many pens on many farms where the great symbol of nature's wildness is raised in pens like chickens.*
◄ *Lilliputian in size next to a hatchery worker, these chinook salmon fry will soon be sent to saltwater net pens.*

◄ *Brad Anderson nets feisty chinook bound for the processing plant, then perhaps the United States or Japan.*
▶ *The net pens of a salmon farm line a bay along British Columbia's Sunshine Coast.*

▶ Before it is lowered into a canal, workers inspect a huge fish screen designed to prevent salmon smolts from being drawn into the irrigation system that taps the Yakima River in Washington state. Before the screens were installed, farmers complained that salmon smolts clogged their sprinkler heads.

WE HAVE POISONED OUR WATER and paved our wetlands, clear-cut our forests and dammed our rivers. We wonder why the salmon runs are disappearing.

▲ Casting a shadow inside a fish screen, a worker checks the outer seals.

▶ Water warmed by a fall drought in 1987 aggravated a once-rare disease, dermocystidium, causing the deaths of hundreds of chinook salmon on the Elwha River in Washington state. The salmon were stacked in a freezer until biologists could examine them. In a natural river, even in a drought, water is cooled by a constant flow from mountains and wetlands. The Elwha has two dams that impede the flow of cool water, warming it. Environmental groups have proposed removing the dams, and Congress has allocated money for studies.

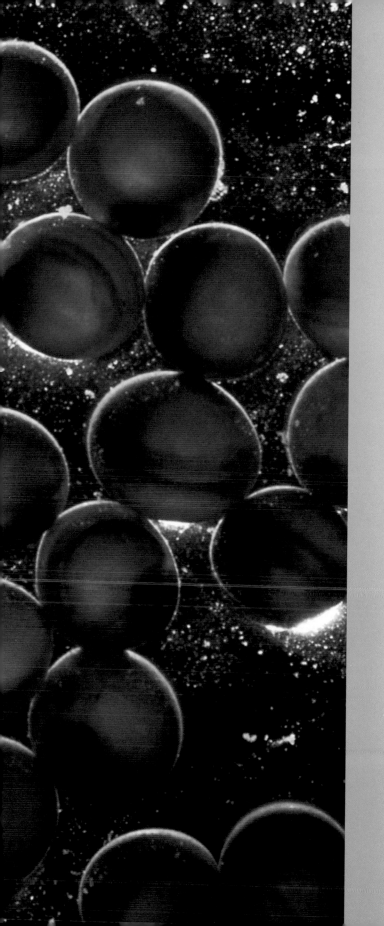

HOMECOMING

Restoration and Return

TOM JAY

IN THE EARLY 1990S, our local salmon restoration group undertook a stock rehabilitation project to rebuild the summer chum runs on two east Olympic Peninsula streams, Salmon and Chimacum creeks, in Washington state. In September, fisheries agents trap chum spawners in a weir and take a percentage of the eggs. These eggs are "eyed up" at the Hurd Creek Hatchery in nearby Sequim and then turned over to us to incubate in a small hatchery we built on a tributary of Salmon Creek. By protecting the eggs, we can boost the egg-to-fry survival by almost 100 percent and hopefully build up the run. We watch the eggs until they hatch, and then feed the fry to a certain size and release them to their sojourn in the sea. Five volunteers alternate checking eggs and fry daily from November to late April. We are committed to this project for at least ten years. We hope to rebuild the Salmon Creek stock first, and then transfer Salmon Creek fish to the chum-barren Chimacum system.

One clear January day I was at our little homemade hatchery checking water temperature and flow, alert for the early hatch that sometimes occurs in a warm winter. I lifted the lid on the incubation barrel to check on the 46,000 eggs, the progeny of twenty wild chum hens, supported by black screened trays and vibrating and rolling delicately in the smooth rhythmic shade of the water flow. It is always a little spooky peering into this watery womb, and I leaned down to study the eggs' opalescent glow. I was trying to decipher what the subtle changes in egg color meant; I was wondering at the dark, sentient density of their eyes. These eggs can see, and that day I had the uncanny sensation that two eggs in particular were watching me. They followed my motions, rolling and twisting to "see" me—it was unnerving. As I closed the incubator lid and began to write up the daily report, I had the eerie intuition that those eggs were the eyes of the watershed, venerable and rejuvenant in the same moment. It was as if 8,000 years of watershed experience—the bio-logic, the patient wisdom of Salmon Creek—were coiled in those two vigilant eggs.

Driving home, my hatchery encounter brought to mind a Fraser River Salish story I'd read years before. In the story, Swanset was married to a woman who was one of the Sockeye Salmon people. Newlywed Swanset lived in his wife's village. Each evening his mother-in-law would come up from the river carrying a salmon in her arms like a child. She

PREVIOUS PAGES:

◄◄ *The journey of the Pacific salmon begins as alevins emerge from their eggs.*
◄ *Less than 1 percent of the millions of eggs laid survive to become spawning adults like these sockeye fighting the shallows of Canada's Weaver Creek.*

► *A Snake River sockeye alevin, listed as an endangered species, is magnified by an electron microscope weeks after it has hatched. In a desperate attempt to save this race of fish from extinction, biologists bred the one female and three males that returned in 1991. This salmon will spend its entire life in a tank to increase its chances of survival. The run was listed as endangered in 1992.*

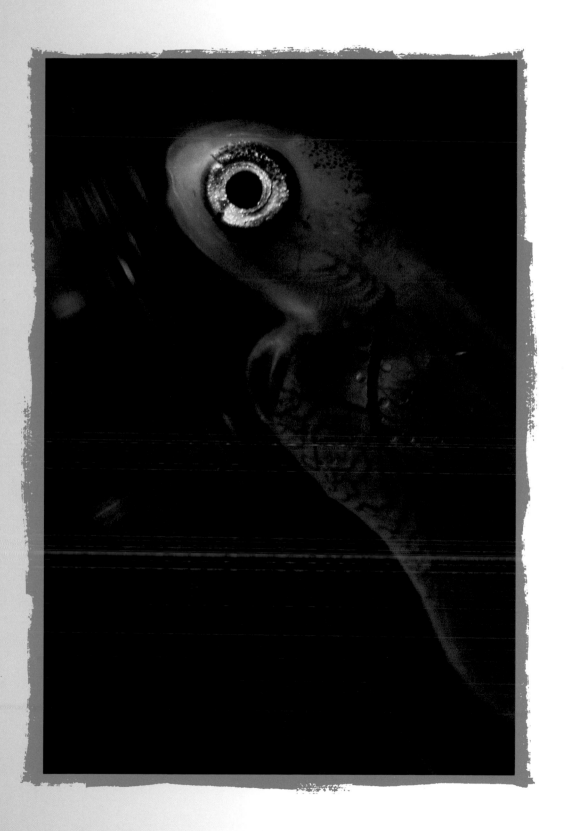

It was unnerving. As I closed the incubator lid and began to write up the daily report, I had the eerie intuition that those eggs were the eyes of the watershed, venerable and rejuvenant in the same moment.

cleaned and cooked it in a respectful way and called Swanset and her daughter to eat. Swanset's wife carefully washed her hands before eating and cautioned Swanset to do likewise. The old matron warned him not to break the salmon bones but to lay them carefully to one side. At meal's end, the mother-in-law gathered up all the bones and returned them to the river. Each evening upon returning the bones and ambling up from the river, stately in the twilight, she was followed by a young boy who rollicked in circles around her. The Sockeye people were glad to see the merry lad; he was vivid witness to the rightness of their way.

Swanset was curious about the miraculous child, and so one evening he kept one of the salmon bones hidden in his mouth. When the boy appeared that evening he was lame, unable to dance and leap. Angry and suspicious, the villagers confronted Swanset. His father-in-law, the chief, threw him to the ground, retrieved the bone, and healed the crippled youngster, who joined them by the fire.

The genius of Native wisdom is to return the bones—to complete the circle and honor the gift by giving back. It is this spirit that blossoms so beautifully in the image of the boy frolicking around the dignified grandmother. Our genius, the industrial trick, is to crack the circle, mine its wealth, and move on. In our contemporary story, the boy doesn't dance but preens sulkily in the rearview mirror of a car, radio blaring, while the grandmother is singing down by the river. The boy is afraid to leave the mirror's enchantment and celebrate her miracle.

Maybe it's as simple as this. In a consumer society, sustenance is a spare transaction: we buy fuel to hurry into the future. For traditional people, food is sacramental and eating is often an act of remembrance and hope. We can't go back to the past and we can't follow our present course into the future. We need a new-old way of looking. Musing on the profound difference between our quick-witted consumer culture and the sustained wisdom of traditional cultures stirs a childhood reminiscence worth retelling.

WE CAN'T GO BACK TO THE PAST AND WE CAN'T FOLLOW OUR PRESENT COURSE INTO THE FUTURE. WE NEED A NEW-OLD WAY OF LOOKING.

◄ *Ainu Shigeru Kayano prepares salmon the old way in a traditional house he built at his cultural museum in the Saru River valley on Hokkaido Island in Japan. The author of several books, he is working to restore fishing rights the Japanese took away at the turn of the century. He uses as a precedent U.S. district court judge George Boldt's 1974 decision allocating half the harvestable salmon to tribes in Washington state. In 1994, Kayano was appointed to a seat in the upper house of the Japanese parliament, a move that may indicate the government is ready to negotiate with the Ainu about fishing and timber rights on their traditional lands. Kayano is the first Ainu to hold this position.*

► *For the first time in forty years, and only as a demonstration for a television show, Ainu were allowed to catch twenty salmon on a stream near Nibutani, Hokkaido, Japan. In a spectacle far from the tradition of honoring each salmon caught, the half-dead fish were brought to the river, placed in a fifty-foot stretch blocked on both ends, and harpooned as they floated belly up.*

WHEN I WAS A CHILD I LOVED MARBLES. I had a big wooden box full of cat's-eyes, aggies, "puries," clay marbles from Mexico, stone marbles from North Carolina. When spring came and the ground had dried, recess would find us racing across the school yard to an old oak tree in whose shade we would draw our circle on the cool clay ground and play.

We laid out our risk marbles, picked our shooters, and lagged to see who would shoot first. Every marble had a meaning and each of our marble bags held an anarchist chess set. The marbles had histories and personalities. Some were heroic, some beautiful, some old and chipped. But all possessed a kind of marble soul. You rolled these marbles around in your hand like a strange seed, a fossil bone or arrowhead.

We played ferociously and hilariously. The best player was a raven-haired girl named Marcia, who hooted and leaped, talking to her marbles like fish in a stream or make-believe grandchildren far from home and in danger. It was a mythic drama we enacted in those dappled green days, a kind of fateful dreaming that required all the qualities adults were coaxing in and out of us in their formal way—daring, skill, practice, strategy, and imagination.

But there was a minority of players who didn't see it as poetically. These players would inevitably propose allowing "steelies" into the game. Steelies are polished steel ball bearings from three-eighths to three-quarters of an inch in diameter. Steelies were a technical fix. They required only good aim and a strong thumb, and whoever went first with a steelie usually won. Other marbles couldn't budge them, and the risk marbles and shooters that were our imaginary friends became fodder in a bottom-line game—win at all costs. Every year we voted steelies out; our game was a theater, a magical circle, not a get-rich-quick scheme. Ever since then the phrase "losing your marbles" as a metaphor for insanity has had a special resonance for me. I think it is the same deep seriousness of that childhood initiation into the

natural heart of culture that inspired thoughtful communities from Japan to Northern California to take responsibility for their local salmon runs. The circle in the clay resounds with the cycle of the salmon; they are both sacred in their way. They protect and inspire us and, broken, further our forsaken spiral into the bottom-line solecism of steelies.

Governments and most businesses play with steelies. They must—we hold them accountable to standards of efficiency, not to those of beauty or soul. They may not save the salmon because they are often distracted by the perennial cacophony of special interests and the pursuit of profit. It is the locals, the neighborhood people, with small circles and vernacular marbles, that are the truest and most useful constituency for the salmon.

What better agents than ourselves to revive our regions' salmon runs? We are the natural kith to their kin. We marvel at the miracle of their return, argue over their health, and rise early to troll and mooch for them in the dark, testy weather of the North Pacific. We ceremoniously savor their firm yet delicate flesh, subtly cooked in a myriad of local and family recipes. In spices, smokes, and sauces, salmon is the soul food of the North Pacific. And while they delight our senses, the salmon also represent us in a profound and heartfelt way. They are the precious mettle of our watersheds. They embody our home places. Salmon are the deep note of our dwelling here, the silver soul of this green bell—steelhead, sockeye, coho, chum, pinks, and kings.

But be warned against restoration romance. Salmon restoration is a paradox more salted with irony than leavened with heroics. Because we assume responsibility does not mean we're in control or will succeed. The salmon know what they're doing. The mind of the "leaper" is tuned to geologic time, and our entropic, superheated civilization may be a minor perturbation in its world. I can imagine salmon of the twentieth millennium spawning in the moonlit rubble of Seattle's Kingdome. Perhaps the question for salmon is how big will civilization grow before it consumes itself? For us the question is, can we get back in sync with

SALMON ARE THE DEEP NOTE OF OUR DWELLING HERE, THE SILVER SOUL OF THIS GREEN BELL— STEELHEAD, SOCKEYE, COHO, CHUM, PINKS, AND KINGS.

◄ *Tulalip Tribe fisheries worker Larry Charley releases wild coho smolts in the Stillaguamish River in Washington state. During a 1987 drought, the salmon had been trapped in shallow pools of the dry riverbed before Larry transported them downstream.*

RESTORATION WORK IS
REALLY REINHABITATION—
COMMUNITY BUILDING WITH
ALL THE "NEIGHBORS."

▶ *Volunteers in Port Hardy, B.C., haul away some of the trash they found while cleaning a salmon stream. Increasingly, community groups and neighborhoods are adopting salmon streams and trying to restore them.*
▶▶ *One of hundreds of endangered Sacramento River chinook salmon that strayed into California irrigation canals is rescued by biologist Jon Polzine for use as brood stock in a hatchery program designed to save the fish. In 1988, biologists were frustrated in their desperate attempt—the eggs had been destroyed by the hot, chemical-laced canal water.*
©*Natalie Fobes / National Geographic Society*

the salmon cycle in time to bank our fires in a suitable hearth? Restoration work is really reinhabitation—community building with all the "neighbors."

IF YOU TRY TO RESTORE SALMON to your watershed, you soon discover the neighborhood is haunted by salmon. The gravel road I drive daily was built decades ago in the middle of a stream: it was the easiest way. Once a small salmon-rich brook, it now trickles half-hearted in ditches on either side of the road. The brook's cycle, the flow, pulse, quality, and quantity of this watershed's water, has been drastically altered not only by misplaced roads but by conversions of forest to pasture and dwellings, short-rotation timber harvest, and

impoundment of this once-spirited rill in ponds that make fish passage impossible. Even if the cutthroat, steelhead, and coho that once returned to this unnamed stream could follow its scent, they could not navigate the tattered threads of its unraveled waters. Following the salmon home is labyrinthian, daunting work.

Revisiting the history of the salmon's decline in our neighborhoods is depressing, but stream work and habitat revival is full of high-spirited comradeship and the small epiphanies of recognition and connection that bloom when what you've done actually works. I recall the chance witness of a coho parr leaping into a culvert we laddered for fish passage two summers ago, the glee with which we greeted one small fry we found in a rill we reconnected to its main stream, and finding a couple of cutthroat fingerlings nestled in the scour pool behind one of the boulders we'd placed in a stream that was downcutting because it had lost structure (wood and stone) and couldn't dissipate its energy. Discrete, vivid moments like these weave us into place. They reconnect us to the complexity and wonder of the natural world, rekindle our imaginations, and edge us away from the unconscious thrall of consumption and back into the quickened drama of creation and community. Restoration then becomes restorying the landscape with tales of its essential beauty.

IMAGINE A THANKSGIVING DINNER of your great-great-grandchildren 100 years from now. In the center of the table is a bright silver salmon locally caught and cooked in the practiced way of long enjoyment and reverence. At the end of the feast there will be a simple ceremony—a long walk to the creek with neighboring families, each with a wooden bowl of salmon bones, to return the remains to the waters of their creation in gratitude and respect. Perhaps there will be mention of the ancestors, if that is who we decide to be—the old ones who stayed put, who gave the salmon shelter in their hearts and who found their own way home.

▶ *On the shore of a Canadian lake, the appearance of salmon skeletons, washed by autumn waves and dried by Indian summer sun, marks the end of the spawning season.*

COMMUNITY
Natalie Fobes

THE COMMUNITY OF PACIFIC SALMON *can still be found along the streams*

and rivers that connect the land to the sea around the Pacific Rim.

For Cathy Fliris, it is a long way from her childhood in suburban Seattle,

with its paved roads and electric lights and grocery stores on every corner.

Her community of salmon is in the heart of Alaska, a day's skiff ride

from the Interior village of Tanana, at a fish camp where she and her

husband, Bill, and their two children spend time between the breakup

and the freezeup of ice on the Yukon River.

They tend a fish wheel, a way of catching fish that has been around since ancient times, and own one of only fifty permits issued for this section of the river. This time of year they don't sell their fish. Neither do their Athabascan neighbors a mile upriver. Nor their Yupik friends downstream. They live a subsistence lifestyle. They live close to the salmon.

PREVIOUS PAGES:

◄ ◄ ◄ *Cathy Fliris hangs split chum salmon to dry on a rack at her family's fish camp on the Yukon River upstream from Tanana, Alaska.*
◄ ◄ *Hanging salmon are dried by the sun and wind of Central Alaska.*

FACING PAGE:

◄ *With morning mists rising around him, Bill Fliris checks his fish wheel on the Yukon River. Salmon are lifted from the water in nets fixed to the paddles of the wheel and dropped into a box on the side.*

▲ *During the peak of the season, Bill empties the box frequently and is often joined by one of his sons.*
◄ *Aaron Kozevnikoff pulls a tote full of salmon to his drying rack at his fish camp a mile upriver from the Flirises'. Of the fifty Yukon fish-wheel subsistence licenses in this region, half are owned by Alaska Natives and half by whites.*

▶ *Many families have traplines that are reachable in the winter only with dog teams. The dogs live on salmon, so part of the fish is dried for their food.*
▶ ▶ *The golden leaves of September warn that winter is on its way. Jesse Fliris wanders down the path to the river.*

THE COMMUNITY OF SALMON can still be found in the dreams of our youth

and in the whispers in our hearts and in the faded memories of a time

before the raging rivers were dammed, the vast forests cut, and the views of

mountains blocked by city skylines. If we try, we will remember when we

lived closer to the earth. We will remember and then we will listen and

hear, and we will wonder why we have journeyed so far from home.

ACKNOWLEDGMENTS

MANY PEOPLE ARE RESPONSIBLE for this book and I want to thank you all. People who helped me find the answers include Tony Floor, Terry Williams, Raymond Moses, Professor Yoshizake, Rollie Schmitten, John Gissberg, Lonnie Selam, and Steve Huffaker. Those who trusted me to tell their stories include Dale Gorman, Molly Gorman, Mary McWithey, Kelly Kerrone, Icicle Seafoods, Brad Larsen, Jimmy Schmidt, Pete Blackwell, Wilbur Slokish, Jr., Leonard Dave, Sr., Darrell Jack, and the Fliris family. Friends who encouraged me through the best and the worst the salmon could give include Scott Sunde, Mary Ann Gwinn, Ann Hopping, Chuck Taylor, Katherine Jones, Fred Nelson, Tom Brown, Celeste Ericsson, Mark Emery, Mark Rosen, Debra Reingold, Geri Migielicz, Don Pugh, Ross Anderson, and Alan Berner. Those who gave me a chance include *National Geographic* editors Tom Kennedy, Bill Garrett, Kent Kobersteen, Dave Arnold, Bob Poole, my editors at *The Seattle Times* including Gary Settle and Alex MacLeod, and the Alicia Patterson Foundation. Those who refused to let the dream die include my agent Elizabeth Wales, editors Ellen Wheat and Marlene Blessing, designer Betty Watson, and writers Brad Matsen and Tom Jay. I am honored by your association. And to Marvin Oliver, whose salmon art graces the pages of this book, my gratitude.

———N. F.

Reinhabitation pioneers Jeremiah Gorsline and Freeman House and salmon realm mentor Jim Lichatowich inspired and tempered my salmon passion. I am enlivened in the fortune of our friendship. Collaborating with Natalie Fobes, Brad Matsen, Ellen Wheat, and Betty Watson had an odd predestined quality, and our efforts joyfully confirmed my admiration for them and the salmon-slippery inevitability of *Reaching Home*. Lastly, gratitude to my wife, Mall Johani, whose honest reflection serves to beacon my mercurial beam.

———T. J.

With great affection, I dedicate my essays in *Reaching Home* to Clem and Diana Tillion of Halibut Cove, Alaska. This book, like all books, is a collaboration, and I am especially indebted to Natalie Fobes, Tom Jay, Ellen Wheat, Marlene Blessing, and Betty Watson who thought salmon with me; and to Holly Hughes and Laara Matsen who supported me, as always, with their love, tolerance, and careful reading.

B. C. M.

These organizations are the umbrella groups for salmon restoration in their regions, and can refer you to the appropriate restoration group in your neighborhood:

CALIFORNIA

Salmonid Restoration Federation
P.O. Box 4260
Arcata, CA 95521
707-444-8903

OREGON

Oregon Restoration and Enhancement Board
P.O. Box 59
Portland, OR 97207
503-229-5410, ext. 323

WASHINGTON

Adopt-a-Stream
P.O. Box 5558
Everett, WA 98206
206-388-3487
Volunteer Fisheries Program
P.O. Box 43136
Olympia, WA 98504-3136
206-902-2260

BRITISH COLUMBIA

Salmonid Enhancement Program
Station 321
555 West Hastings Street
Vancouver, BC V6B 5G3
604-666-6285

ALASKA

Habitat Restoration Division
Dept. of Fish and Game
P.O. Box 240020
Douglas, AK 99824
907-465-4290

JAPAN

Come Back Salmon Society
Hokkaido, Japan

FURTHER READING

American Friends Service Committee. *Uncommon Controversy: Fishing Rights of Muckleshoot, Puyallup and Nisqually Indians.* Seattle: University of Washington Press, 1970.

Boas, Franz. *Tsimshian Mythology.* Chicago: University of Chicago Press, 1916.

Brown, Bruce. *Mountain in the Clouds: A Search for the Wild Salmon.* New York: Simon and Schuster, 1982.

Caras, Roger. *Sockeye: The Life of the Pacific Salmon.* New York: Dial Press, 1975.

Childerhose, R. J., and Marj Trim. *Pacific Salmon and Steelhead Trout.* Seattle: University of Washington Press, 1979.

Clark, Ella E. *Indian Legends of the Pacific Northwest.* Berkeley: University of California Press, 1953.

Cohen, Fay G. *Treaties on Trial.* Seattle: University of Washington Press, 1986.

Crandall, Julie V. *The Story of the Pacific Salmon.* Portland, Ore.: Binfords and Mort, 1946.

Dore, Ian. *Salmon, the Illustrated Handbook for Commercial Users.* New York: Van Nostrand Reinhold, 1990.

Fobes, Natalie, photographer. "The Long Journey of the Pacific Salmon." *National Geographic,* July 1990.

———. "The Saga of Salmon." *The Seattle Times,* November 22, 1987. 12-page special insert.

Freeburn, Laurence, ed. *The Silver Years of the Alaska Canned Salmon Industry.* Anchorage: Alaska Northwest Books, 1976.

Gorsline, Jeremiah. "Shadows of Our Ancestors." *Readings in The History of Klallam-White Relations.* Port Townsend, Wash.: Empty Bowl Press, 1992.

———, and Finn Wilcox, eds. *Working the Woods, Working the Sea: An Anthology of Northwest Writings.* Port Townsend, Wash.: Empty Bowl Press, 1986.

Groot, C., and L. Margolis, eds. *Pacific Salmon Life Histories.* Vancouver, B.C.: University of British Columbia Press, 1991.

Gunther, Erna. *Klallam Folk Tales.* Seattle: University of Washington Press, 1923.

———. *Klallam Ethnography.* Seattle: University of Washington Press, 1927.

———. *A Further Analysis of the First Salmon Ceremony.* Seattle: University of Washington Press, 1930.

———. *Art in the Life of the Northwest Coast Indians.* Seattle: Superior Publishing Company, 1966.

Hart, J. L. *Pacific Fishes of Canada.* Ottawa: Fisheries Research Board of Canada, 1973.

House, Linn. "Totem Salmon." *Truck 18, Biogeography Workbook No. 1.* St. Paul, Minn.: Truck Press, 1978.

Jay, Tom. "Salmon of the Heart." *Working the Woods, Working the Sea: An Anthology of Northwest Writings.* Port Townsend, Wash.: Empty Bowl Press, 1986.

———. "The Salmon of the Heart." *Orion,* Autumn 1992.

Johnson, Paul C. *The Scientific Angler.* New York: Scribners, 1984.

Koo, Ted S. Y., ed. *Studies of Alaska Red Salmon.* Seattle: University of Washington Press, 1962.

McKeown, Brian A. *Fish Migration.* Portland, Ore.: Timber Press, 1984.

McKervill, Hugh W. *The Salmon People.* Vancouver, B.C.: Whitecap Books, 1992.

Netboy, Anthony. *Salmon of the Pacific Northwest.* Portland, Ore.: Binfords and Mort, 1958.

———. *The Salmon, Their Fight for Survival.* Boston: Houghton Mifflin Company, 1973.

———. *The Columbia River Salmon and Steelhead Trout.* Seattle: University of Washington Press, 1980.

———. *Salmon, the World's Most Harassed Fish.* Tulsa, Okla.: Winchester Press, 1980.

Ommanney, F. D. *A Draught of Fishes.* New York: Thomas Crowell Co., 1966.

Sakurai, Atsushi. *Salmon.* New York: Alfred Knopf, 1984.

Smith, Courtland L. *Salmon Fishers of the Columbia.* Corvallis: Oregon State University Press, 1979.

Steelquist, Robert. *Field Guide to the Pacific Salmon.* Seattle: Sasquatch Books, 1992.

Troll, Ray, and Brad Matsen. *Ray Troll's Shocking Fish Tales.* Seattle: Alaska Northwest Books, 1991.

Vannote, Robin. *The River Continuum: A Theoretical Construct for Analysis of River Systems.* Contribution #1 from NSF River Continuum Project, Stroud Water Research Center, Academy of Natural Sciences of Philadelphia, 1984.

Wallace, David Rains. *Life in the Balance.* San Diego: Harcourt Brace Jovanovich, 1987.

Watanabe, Hitoshi. *The Ainu Ecosystem.* Seattle: University of Washington Press, 1972.

Wright, Robin K., ed. *A Time of Gathering.* Seattle: Burke Museum and University of Washington Press, 1991.

INDEX

INDEX